The Excellent Online Instructor

The Excellent Online Instructor

STRATEGIES FOR PROFESSIONAL DEVELOPMENT

Rena M. Palloff
Keith Pratt

JOSSEY-BASS
A Wiley Imprint
www.josseybass.com

Published by Jossey-Bass
A Wiley Imprint
989 Market Street, San Francisco, CA 94103-1741—www.josseybass.com

Readers should be aware that Internet Web sites offered as citations and/or sources for further information may have changed or disappeared between the time this was written and when it is read.

Limit of Liability/Disclaimer of Warranty: While the publisher and author have used their best efforts in preparing this book, they make no representations or warranties with respect to the accuracy or completeness of the contents of this book and specifically disclaim any implied warranties of merchantability or fitness for a particular purpose. No warranty may be created or extended by sales representatives or written sales materials. The advice and strategies contained herein may not be suitable for your situation. You should consult with a professional where appropriate. Neither the publisher nor author shall be liable for any loss of profit or any other commercial damages, including but not limited to special, incidental, consequential, or other damages.

Jossey-Bass books and products are available through most bookstores. To contact Jossey-Bass directly call our Customer Care Department within the U.S. at 800-956-7739, outside the U.S. at 317-572-3986, or fax 317-572-4002.

Jossey-Bass also publishes its books in a variety of electronic formats. Some content that appears in print may not be available in electronic books.

Library of Congress Cataloging-in-Publication Data
Palloff, Rena M., 1950-
  The Excellent Online Instructor : Strategies for Professional Development / Rena M. Palloff, Keith Pratt.
    p. cm. –
  Includes bibliographical references and index.
  ISBN 978-0-470-63523-0 (pbk.)
      978-1-118-00088-5 (ebk)
      978-1-118-00089-2 (ebk)
      978-1-118-00090-8 (ebk)

  1. Web-based instruction. 2. Computer-assisted instruction. 3. Distance education. 4. Effective teaching. I. Title.
  LB1044.87.P338 2011
  371.33′44678—dc22

                                                                    2010045578

Printed in the United States of America
FIRST EDITION

PB Printing
10 9 8 7 6 5 4 3 2 1

CONTENTS

V

LIST OF FIGURES AND TABLES

FIGURES

TABLES

In September 2005, Hurricane Katrina struck the Gulf Coast and city of New Orleans. The levees breached and the city was flooded. Delgado Community College lost 70% of its physical plant as a result of the storm, but the server that housed Blackboard, the college's course management system, was on dry ground and functioning. In order to be able to hold some form of a fall semester that would reach Delgado students and engage Delgado faculty, most of whom were scattered all over the United States, the college moved many courses online. With only three days to prepare, Delgado launched a major online initiative. When the floodwaters receded and the fall semester came to an end, the college realized that this piecemeal approach to online teaching wouldn't work in the long run and they began a faculty training effort that continues today. What started with just enough technical training to get courses on Blackboard has morphed into a continuous quality improvement effort focusing on effective online pedagogy.

As of this writing, it is fall 2009 and the H1N1 flu virus is significantly impacting college campuses. The response of many academic institutions is to ask their faculty to prepare to go online—that preparation, for the most part, involves technical instruction on using lecture capture technologies, basics on using Blackboard and other course management systems, using Microsoft Office effectively as a means of sharing documents with students, and so forth. Little to no attention is being paid to what makes online teaching effective—only what can be done in a pinch to get course material online so that students or faculty who are ill can continue to be involved in classes. But what about those faculty whose institutions are not providing such training? How will they prepare? Will they be able to deliver material online if they have not had this experience previously? And will this effort result in a greater effort to provide effective online classes, as happened at Delgado? Although we would love to believe that the Delgado experience is the norm, we are less optimistic given the state of faculty development for online teaching as it exists today.

Recently we conducted several workshops on the topic of online faculty development. What was most interesting to us was that the participants strongly echoed a common theme—we need to get back to basics when training online faculty. What prompted this felt need? The participants cited several reasons, including

- Faculty are rarely given the level of training and support they need to begin teaching online, if given training at all, resulting in confusion about how to get started.

- Training continues to be focused on the technology in use instead of how to teach in the online environment, resulting in confusion about what to do once the online course begins.

- Faculty are busy and often do not participate fully in training.

- Faculty lack familiarity with the tools of online teaching.

- Often faculty are brought in last-minute to teach a section of a course online and are thrown in with little to no training.

- Faculty training takes too much time—time that administrators see as wasted time, time they do not wish to pay for, or time not well spent.

- Faculty resist mandatory training—is there a way to make exceptions for seasoned faculty? Can we honor experience somehow?

- Although a constructivist approach is generally promoted as the most effective means by which to deliver a course online, faculty resist constructivist approaches to training.

- Training should not be a one-shot experience but should be ongoing.

- The goals of training are rarely clear—what is it that the institution and students need in order to create an excellent teaching and learning experience?
- What about institutions that don't even offer training? What do faculty do there to get up to speed so that they can teach online?

Although we have discussed the need for good faculty training that explores best practices in online teaching rather than the use of technology online, and the demand for online teaching is well documented and continues to grow (Allen & Seaman, 2007), the training of online instructors has not kept pace with the demand for excellence in the online environment, a demand voiced by students and administrators alike. The result has been poorly constructed courses, high levels of student attrition from online courses, and continued allegations that online education is simply not as rigorous as its face-to-face counterpart. Furthermore, faculty are often left on their own to find appropriate training or to create their own approach to online teaching based on conversations with colleagues or information they find online or in journals.

There is no doubt that online education continues to grow. Two-year, four-year, graduate programs, and fully online institutions are all offering online classes in increasing numbers, but the availability of trained faculty to teach these courses continues to be a critical issue across the board. Faculty are rarely provided with training in the pedagogical skills they need to teach online. A 2002 survey of faculty who teach in various disciplines and are located throughout the United States yielded results that appear to be the norm of faculty experience, as 75% indicated that they had received approximately 30 hours of technical training in the course management system they would be using; however, only one-third reported receiving any pedagogical training. A subset of surveyed faculty were interviewed; they described the difficulties they were having engaging students in online discussion and their perceived need for pedagogical training (Pankowski, 2004). We contend, however, that with attention to good training and development, faculty excellence in the online environment can be achieved. The result of excellent course development and delivery would be increased student persistence in online courses and strong course outcomes. The intent of this book is to help faculty who teach online and those who are responsible for their training and development achieve that level of excellence. What, then, makes a successful online instructor and how can excellent instructors be trained and developed? How can faculty become their own trainers–developers to help achieve a goal of excellence in online teaching? These are the central questions that will be explored and addressed in this book.

ABOUT THIS BOOK

This book is aimed at three audiences. Primarily it is for and about faculty—faculty who are moving into the online environment for the first time or faculty who seek to improve their online teaching practice. In addition, the book is designed to assist faculty developers, as well as those faculty who have been asked to train their peers, to design and deliver effective training for online teaching. Finally, the book is directed at administrators who supervise and evaluate faculty performance in online teaching. Good instructors and instruction are the strongest marketing tools an online course or program can have. Because research evidence suggests that a good instructor is the key to student persistence in online courses, the hiring, training, and evaluation of good online instructors has become high priority for most online institutions. With increasing scale of online class delivery, however, comes the need to recruit and hire faculty who may not have the experience or skills coming into an online course or program that they need. Consequently, providing good training and also providing incentives for keeping good faculty have become critical concerns. Our own experience of training online faculty using an online learning community has shown us that this is a very effective means by which to prepare faculty for online course development and delivery. This book will help readers

- Identify faculty who will be effective in the online environment and assess their readiness to teach online
- Know what it takes to develop a new instructor in order to promote excellent online teaching
- Describe the qualities of a good online instructor and how to evaluate good teaching online
- Develop good models of faculty training for online teaching based on adult learning principles and best practices in faculty training
- Identify methods and processes that have shown to be successful in training and motivating online instructors
- Identify means by which technology can be used to facilitate and enhance the training process

- Identify best practices that exemplify excellence in online teaching
- Identify means by which faculty can engage in their own training and development to supplement what is being offered by their institutions or replace it if none is offered

Models of effective faculty training and evaluation will be reviewed along with strategies for retaining good faculty and building faculty loyalty to the institution. We also address K–12 educators in this book. The demand for technology integration and online classes in the K–12 sector is also growing and, in many cases, is better structured and funded than it is in the community colleges or higher education. Mentoring has been a practice that has been a standard in teacher development, but is not widely applied for online teaching in higher education. Thus, professional development for teachers is becoming a powerful force and may, in fact, offer models for higher education to follow.

We recognize that training, if offered, continues to focus on the use of technology when faculty are clamoring for more and better information about how to actually teach in the online environment. Although we do not explore specific strategies and suggestions for teaching online, as we have in our other books, in this book we explore ways in which faculty can find and use resources that can assist them in the development of those strategies. In so doing, this book also addresses the need of faculty members who are designated as the coordinator of faculty training or distance learning on their campuses, but who may not be trained faculty developers themselves, to point their faculty colleagues in the right direction. It also provides a means by which faculty can work collaboratively to support one another as they explore what may be unchartered territory for them.

Providing training for faculty in order to help them get started and also to support their ongoing work in online teaching helps. Providing training online through the development of an online learning community for faculty can be even more powerful and effective. And finally, providing faculty with ideas they can use to support their own development may be the ideal, given budgetary constraints and the absence of institutional support. Numerous models exist to support this effort—none is the one "right" way to train faculty—and the review and evaluation of those is an important part of this book. The goal is to develop and present approaches that will not only get the job done, in terms of teaching faculty how to teach online, but also that will develop faculty excellence in online teaching. Excellent online faculty attract students to courses and programs and help retain those students. Excellent online faculty also help improve the quality and rigor of the courses they teach. We intend, through this book, to encourage institutions not just to train faculty to do online work but also to promote excellence. We also intend to encourage faculty to seek excellence in their online teaching, whether or not their institutions support them through the provision of training in doing so.

ORGANIZATION OF CONTENTS

This book is divided into three parts and ends with several resources to support the work of faculty, faculty developers, and administrators in pursuit of good faculty development and evaluation. Each chapter ends with a review of key points made in the chapter along with tips for the instructor who wishes to pursue training on his or her own to help maximize the benefits of training oneself. The sections, entitled Becoming Your Own Faculty Developer, will include resources and suggestions for self-development as an excellent online instructor.

Part One provides the groundwork for the book by focusing on the characteristics of the excellent online instructor in Chapter One, how that instructor develops over time in Chapter Two, and the elements of good training in Chapter Three. This part of the book emphasizes the importance of incorporating adult learning theory into training, as well as working with the competencies and experience a faculty member already possesses. In addition, an overarching focus of Part One will be faculty readiness—How can that be assessed and how can we incorporate factors related to readiness into training?

Part Two of the book looks at more specific topics related to faculty development. Chapter Four looks at the various models employed to train and develop faculty, suggests the most effective techniques and strategies for faculty development, and looks at a common question—Is face-to-face training more effective than online training? The benefit of both, along with exploration of hybrid models, is explored in this chapter. Chapter Five looks at the important topic of mentoring and its role in faculty development for online teaching. Formal mentoring programs are reviewed along with suggestions for the development of both formal and informal mentoring approaches. Chapter Six is devoted to the topic of professional development in the K–12 sector and includes a review of what is currently being offered there along with suggestions for closing the gap between teacher education and K–12 online teaching.

Part Three connects faculty development with faculty evaluation. Chapter Seven looks specifically at this topic and suggests means by which administrators or those responsible for faculty evaluation can most effectively connect training and development to evaluation tasks, with the desired outcome that the results of evaluation should drive training. Suggestions include ways to involve faculty in their own evaluation, as well as peer evaluation. Chapter Eight closes the book by speaking to each of the three audiences for whom the book was written, pulling together ideas on best practices in faculty development and evaluation and proposing a best practices model that readers can adopt or adapt for their own institutions.

Finally, three resources are provided—one for faculty developers or those tasked with coordinating faculty development on their campuses, a second for faculty to support them in their own development, and a third for administrators or those who conduct faculty evaluation and who develop training programs for faculty.

WHO WILL BENEFIT FROM READING THIS BOOK?

The primary audience for this book is higher education professionals, including faculty engaged in online teaching, as well as instructional designers and other academic support staff involved in the development, design, and facilitation of online courses and training and support of online instructors. An additional primary audience includes other professionals in higher education who oversee the training and evaluation function of online instructors, such as faculty who are designated as the coordinators of faculty development or distance learning and may or may not be prepared to do so, as well as those charged with professional development in the K–12 sector. Department chairs, deans, and other administrators who are responsible for faculty evaluation will constitute yet another audience for the book. They will benefit not only from the suggestions about what constitutes good training but also how to link training to evaluation in order to create a comprehensive system that makes sense to them and to the faculty being evaluated.

It is our hope that this book will positively influence the direction of training and development for online teaching. Although we advocate for the provision of extensive training on every campus, we realize that difficult financial times makes this almost impossible. We firmly believe, however, that by taking our suggestions for self-training and development to heart, faculty can become their own best asset in their quest for excellence. We further hope that all faculty who read this book and follow our suggestions to improve their online teaching practice will pay their positive experiences forward by becoming a resource to their colleagues. Working together collaboratively and thus forming a community of practice not only benefits faculty but also pays enormous dividends to our students as they experience effective, excellent instruction. This, in turn, will have the impact of improving online instruction as a whole. It's a big dream, but not out of reach.

ACKNOWLEDGMENTS

This book is for all the faculty who have worked with us in our online classes and programs, workshops, and training seminars—thank you for making your needs known and for seeking excellence for yourselves. We hope that this book supports you on your journey.

Once again, we have to thank the patient, supportive, and dedicated people at Jossey-Bass. Thanks in particular to Erin Null and David Brightman—we so appreciate you both! Thanks also to Jessica Egbert for pushing us to write this one and make this contribution to the field of online learning.

We always have to thank Fielding Graduate University and Judy Witt, the Dean of the School of Educational Leadership and Change, for support of the Teaching in the Virtual Classroom Program. The program gives us an opportunity to work with very talented instructors who are interested in nothing more than seeking excellence in their own online work. Mostly, we thank our participants—the "students" in the TVC program for their contributions to our ongoing learning. Virtual hugs to you all! We cannot thank you enough.

Thanks, of course, to our families—your patience and love is what helps us do what we do and pushes us to seek our own level of excellence.

THE AUTHORS

Rena M. Palloff is a managing partner of Crossroads Consulting Group, working with institutions, organizations, and corporations interested in the development of online distance learning and training programs and conducting faculty development training and coaching. In addition, Rena has consulted extensively in health care, academic settings, and addiction treatment for well over twenty years. Rena is faculty at Fielding Graduate University, in the masters' degree program in Organizational Management and Development and also in the School of Educational Leadership and Change. She is also adjunct faculty at Capella University in the School of Public Service Leadership. Additionally, she has taught classes on organizational behavior and management and leadership on an adjunct basis for the International Studies Program at Ottawa University in Ottawa, Kansas, in various sites throughout the Pacific Rim, and was core faculty at John F. Kennedy University in Holistic Studies.

Dr. Palloff received a bachelors degree in sociology from the University of Wisconsin-Madison and a masters degree in social work from the University of Wisconsin-Milwaukee. She holds a masters degree in organizational development and a Ph.D. in human and organizational systems from Fielding Graduate University.

Keith Pratt began his government career as a computer systems technician with the U.S. Air Force in 1967. He served in various positions, including supervisor of computer systems maintenance, chief of the Logistics Support Branch, chief of the Telecommunications Branch, and superintendent of the Secure Telecommunications Branch. After leaving the Air Force, Pratt held positions as registrar and faculty (Charter College), director (Chapman College), and trainer and consultant (The Growth Company). As an adjunct faculty member at Wayland Baptist University and at the University of Alaska, Pratt taught courses in communications, business, management, organizational theories, and computer technology. He was assistant professor in the International Studies Program and chair of the Management Information Systems Program, main campus and overseas, at Ottawa University in Ottawa, Kansas. He currently teaches online at Fielding Graduate University, Wayland Baptist University, Capella University, and Walden University.

Pratt graduated from Wayland Baptist University with a dual degree in business administration and computer systems technology. He has an M.S. in human resource management (with honors) from Chapman University, an M.S. in organizational development, a Ph.D. in human and organizational systems from Fielding Graduate University, and an honorary doctorate of science from Moscow State University.

Palloff and Pratt are managing partners in Crossroads Consulting Group. Since 1994, they have collaboratively conducted pioneering research and training in the emerging areas of online group facilitation, face-to-face and online community building, program planning and development of distance learning programs, and management and supervision of online academic programs. In conjunction with Fielding Graduate University, they developed and are core faculty in the Teaching in the Virtual Classroom academic certificate program designed to assist faculty in becoming effective online facilitators and course developers.

PART ONE

The Excellent
Online Instructor

What Are the Characteristics of Excellent Online Teaching?

There is a myth that has existed in the world of online teaching since it began. The myth asserts that it is easy to teach online—all one needs to do is to move exactly what was being done in the face-to-face classroom into the online classroom. Technologies such as lecture capture video and PowerPoint have made it easy for an instructor to lecture online, and simply writing up and posting assignments by copying and pasting into the course management system in use is not difficult. But can this be considered good instruction online?

There are a significant number of instructors who are sincerely interested in online education and its possibilities. Early enthusiasts explored alternative ways of teaching in this environment and became champions for this form of teaching and learning, encouraging others to join them in new and exciting ways of delivering courses. However, some instructors have been told that they *must* develop and teach online classes. They are being given no choice in the matter and are reluctantly entering the online environment. Many feel lost, not even sure where to begin. Others have heard and believe the myth that the key to success is content; simply migrate the content that has been taught in the face-to-face classroom into the online classroom, and all will be well. Others learn how to use the software that is designed to teach the course and think that this is all they need to know to move successfully to the online environment. Yet others simply set up a course and then virtually "walk away," leaving students to fend for themselves with little guidance or direction. In many cases, instructors receive little to no guidance in how to teach online and are thus put in a position of fending for themselves, requiring them to learn not only the course management system in use but also how to facilitate an online course on their own. In yet other situations, a faculty member who may have some technological knowledge or expertise may be put in charge of the university's faculty development effort in addition to continuing with his or her own course load—often these faculty members have little to no knowledge of how to conduct good faculty development and consequently have an additional teaching and self-training burden added to their load.

The result of these false assumptions is often the development of courses that are poorly conceived and lack interactivity, taught by faculty who are frustrated by their inability to get students involved. A likely outcome is low enrollment or attrition from online courses and programs. Akridge, DeMay, Braunlich, Collura, and Sheahan (2002) suggest that student retention online is dependent on three factors: selecting the right students for the right program; using a highly learner-focused delivery model; and engaging learners at a personal level. Hebert (2006) discovered that the responsiveness of faculty to perceived student needs helps increase persistence in online courses and creates a greater degree of satisfaction with the learning process. In other words, good instructors and instruction are the strongest marketing tools an online program can have. Because research evidence suggests that a good instructor is the key to student persistence in online courses, the hiring, training, and evaluation of good online instructors should be high priority for most online institutions. With scale, however, comes the need to recruit and hire faculty who may not have the experience or skills coming into an online course or program that they need. Consequently, providing good training and also providing incentives for keeping good faculty have become critical concerns. Difficult economic times, however, have taken their toll on faculty training—when budgets need to be cut, faculty development is the first to go, leaving more and more online instructors in a position to either go without training or find a way to train themselves.

These are essential components of what it takes to teach online, and yet if faculty are only receiving technical training before they embark on teaching their first online course, how would they know how to do this? What makes a successful online instructor and how can excellent instructors be trained? This is the central question that will be explored and addressed in this book. All is not lost in terms of online faculty development and the potential emergence of excellent online instructors, despite the obstacles facing them. There are many resources now available to the online instructor left to his or her own devices to receive good training or for the faculty member who has been tapped to provide training to his or her peers. This book is designed to be one of those resources. By exploring what makes an excellent online instructor, how to conduct effective training, and how to do it for oneself if the institution is not, we believe that faculty can strive for and achieve excellence in their online teaching.

WHAT DOES THE EXCELLENT ONLINE INSTRUCTOR LOOK LIKE?

The growing popularity of online instruction has brought with it increasing recognition that teaching online differs from face-to-face teaching. As a result, more attention is being paid to what constitutes positive educational experiences online and the characteristics of good online instructors and courses. Organizations such as Quality Matters have emerged that are designed to evaluate online course design, and faculty at many institutions are being trained as Quality Matters evaluators so as to determine the quality of courses being designed by their peers and to offer suggestions for improvement. In addition, other institutions, such as California State University–Chico (Rubric for Online Instruction) and the Illinois Online Network (Quality Online Course Initiative Rubric) have published course design rubrics that are available online for anyone who wants to evaluate his or her own course. These can also be used as components of the evaluation of good course design and online teaching practice. Like the Quality Matters rubric, the CSU-Chico rubric focuses primarily on good design elements. The Illinois Online Network QOCI, however, does look at elements that promote collaboration between students and interaction between student and instructor.

In one of our previous books (Palloff & Pratt, 2003), we noted that much of the literature on best practices in online teaching was limited to the effective use of various technologies. Since that time, however, more attention has been paid to what constitutes best practice in online instruction. This aligns closely with our discussion of Graham, Kursat, Byung-Ro, Craner, and Duffy's (2001) article linking the Chickering and Gamson (1987) Seven Principles of Good Practice in Undergraduate Education to online teaching. Graham et al. note the following seven lessons for online instruction: Instructors should provide clear guidelines for interaction with students; provide well-designed discussion assignments to promote cooperation among students; encourage students to present course projects to one another; provide prompt feedback of two types—information and acknowledgment; provide assignment deadlines; provide challenging tasks, sample cases, and praise for high-quality work to reinforce high expectations; and allow students to choose project topics.

Based on Weimer's (2002) work on learner-focused teaching, in order to achieve all of this, we note that several things need to happen:

- The balance of power needs to change—The instructor online acts as a learning facilitator, allowing students to take charge of their own learning process.

- The function of content needs to change—As noted by Carr-Chellman and Duchastel (2001), good online course design makes learning resources and instructional activities available to students rather than providing instruction in the form of a lecture or other means.

- The role of the instructor needs to change—by establishing active and strong online presence, a topic we will return to in more depth, the instructor demonstrates his or her expertise and guides the students in their learning process.

- The responsibility for learning needs to change—with the instructor acting as guide, resource, and facilitator, students need to take more responsibility for their own learning process.

- The purpose and process of assessment and evaluation need to change—traditional means of assessment, such as tests and quizzes, do not always meet the mark when it comes to this form of learning. Consequently, other forms of assessment, such as self-assessment and application activities, should be incorporated to assess student learning and evaluate areas for potential course improvement (Palloff & Pratt, 2003).

What we have been discussing here is what good facilitation looks like in an online course. But how does this translate into the characteristics of the excellent online instructor? And are the same characteristics required regardless of the level at which the online course is offered: K–12 through graduate level? An issue-oriented white paper that was published following a conference on virtual pedagogy (Kircher, 2001) offered the following characteristics: organized; highly motivated and enthusiastic; committed to teaching; supports student-centered learning; open to suggestions; creative; takes risks; manages time well; responsive to learner needs; disciplined; and is interested in online delivery without expectation of other rewards. Savery (2005) offers the VOCAL acronym to describe the effective online instructor. In other words, the effective online instructor is Visible, Organized, Compassionate, Analytical, and a Leader by example. The Illinois Online Network (2007) adds to the list by noting that good online instructors have a broad base of life experience in addition to their teaching credentials; demonstrate openness, concern, flexibility, and sincerity (characteristics we have consistently equated with online excellence); feel comfortable communicating in writing (a characteristic also stressed by Kearsley, n.d.); accept that the facilitated model of teaching is equally powerful to traditional teaching methods; value critical thinking; and is experienced and well-trained in online teaching. Kearsley (n.d.) also notes that having experienced online instruction as a student also helps, something that we support wholeheartedly. Clearly, it is this last component—well trained in online instruction—that we will be emphasizing in this book and we contend that regardless of the educational level of the student enrolled in the online class, this is the key to excellence. Before we embark on that exploration, however, we want to delve further into a few areas that we feel are significant in the emergence of excellence online—the ability to establish presence, create and maintain a learning community, and effectively develop and facilitate online courses.

THE IMPORTANCE OF ESTABLISHING PRESENCE

Establishing presence is the first order of business in an online class, and the ability of the instructor to do so effectively, as well as to be able to encourage its development among the students, is one measure of instructor excellence online. Establishing presence is the process of demonstrating to others who we are in the online environment, as well as making social connections with others who share that environment with us. It is the concept of visibility as described by Savery (2005) and is critical to students in perceiving that the instructor is paying attention to them and to their learning needs. In addition, Savery notes that when students are able to establish their own sense of presence, instructors are assured that they are attending to the learning tasks that are part of the course.

Establishing presence is something we rarely consider when teaching face-to-face. In that setting, students can see and hear us, as well as see and hear one another. To some degree, they will establish a sense of who their instructor and colleagues are simply by being in the same physical space, although Picciano (2002) warns that this doesn't always happen without effort. Online, however, an effort to establish presence is always needed. "Online there is greater possibility for a sense of loss among learners—loss of contact, loss of connection, and a resultant sense of isolation. Consequently, attention should be paid to the intentional development of presence" (Palloff & Pratt, 2007, p. 31).

Savery (2005) discusses means by which presence can be established online, including the instructor's development and maintenance of a website that outlines both personal and professional information, responses in discussion forums that indicate that posts are being read, e-mail messages to the class on various topics, as well as announcements and banners on the homepage of the course, keeping a shared calendar, and possible use of audio and video clips. We add to this list the use of synchronous media, such as Skype (an application that allows for online conference calling along with chat, a whiteboard, etc.) or virtual classroom technologies (such as WebEx, Elluminate, or Adobe Connect that provide online classroom spaces to be accessed in real time), so that students can hear the instructor and each other, instructor blogs (or Web Logs, allowing the instructor or students to keep online journals), and the use of social networking technologies such as Facebook and Twitter to share updates of both personal and professional nature. Although we are not currently teaching in Second Life (a virtual world that allows for simulation), many instructors feel that this, too, adds to a sense of presence, even with the use of avatars that may or may not represent the participants outside of the virtual world.

The intent is to create a sense of connection with learners who are otherwise separated by time and space. In so doing, the level of interaction in the online course increases—when social presence is low, interaction also is low and vice versa (Stein & Wanstreet, 2003). Presence is associated with effective instruction online (Gunawardena, 1995), greater depth of learning (Picciano, 2002; Richardson & Swan, 2003; Rovai & Barnum, 2003), and learner satisfaction with the online learning process (Gunawardena & Zittle, 1997; Rovai & Barnum, 2003). The ability to create presence as a marker of instructor excellence and how to incorporate this into faculty development is a topic we return to in Chapter Two and later in the book.

ENGAGING LEARNERS AND CREATING COMMUNITY

The ability to establish presence is closely connected to the ability of the instructor to create a sense of community among the learners in an online course. Picciano (2002) notes that a sense of social presence correlates to a sense of belonging to a learning community, and Garrison, Anderson, and Archer (2003), as we do, identify it as a precursor to the development of community. Wenger (1999) notes that the social aspects of education are the most important and need attention before delving into the exploration of content. In the online environment, attention to the social aspects of engagement become more difficult. As we have noted in our extensive discussions of the creation of community, the establishment of that community satisfies a need to belong, reduces learner isolation, enhances learning outcomes, and creates a shared goal for learning. Brook and Oliver (2003) concluded after an extensive review of the existing literature on the online learning community, "There is strong support for the supposition that the social phenomenon of community may be put to good use in the support of online learning. This is well supported by theories of learning that highlight the role of social interaction in the construction of knowledge" (p. 150). Charalambos, Michalinos, and Chamberlain (2004) describe what they believe to be the common characteristics of the learning community, which include a common sense of responsibility among participants toward assigned tasks and their peers; joint vision and control of the community equally shared among members; a safe environment where opinions can be freely shared and questions asked without fear of retribution; structural dependence that establishes the need to interact and share resources; and mutual support among members and subgroups.

The learning community, then, becomes the vehicle through which the course is effectively conducted (Palloff & Pratt, 2005, 2007). "By learning together in a learning community, students have the opportunity to extend and deepen their learning experience, test out new ideas by sharing them with a supportive group, and receive critical and constructive feedback" (Palloff & Pratt, 2005, p. 8). Measurable outcomes of community formation include active interaction regarding course content and on a personal level, attempts at collaborative learning evidenced by increasing learner-to-learner interaction, socially constructed meaning evidenced by questioning and agreement on issues of content and meaning, active sharing of resources among learners, expressions of support and encouragement between learners along with a willingness to constructively critique the work of others (Palloff & Pratt, 2007).

This discussion begs the question: How does this correlate with instructor excellence when the focus is on the connection between learners? An excellent online instructor will know how to get the process started, facilitate it effectively, and then get out of the way and observe the results, jumping in as a resource to share expertise when necessary and to guide the process. Instructors who are new to the online environment may struggle with the transition from the central figure in the learning process to a facilitator or guide of that process. Making that transition is a topic we discuss in more depth in Chapter Two when we talk about the process of faculty development for online instruction and again in Chapter Three when we discuss training techniques. For the purpose of this discussion, however, it is important to note that a sign of instructor excellence online is evidence of the elements that we feel are essential to the creation of the online learning community—the willingness to give up control of the process to the learners and empower them to take charge of the learning process, demonstration of presence through responsiveness and respectful clear communication using various means, and the development and delivery of an instructional design that allows all of this to happen. It is to this last topic that we now turn our attention.

EXCELLENCE IN COURSE DEVELOPMENT

How do we evaluate effective online courses and how can this become an indicator of excellence in online teaching? One important response to this question has been the development and application of the Quality Matters Rubric. Based on extensive and continuous review of the literature on the topic of effective online course design, Quality Matters, developed by the University of Maryland, uses a peer evaluation approach to the determination of effectiveness and to offer suggestions for quality improvement in courses. The focus is on course development rather than the delivery and facilitation of the course based on the important precept that good design is critical to good delivery. The rubric used by Quality Matters looks at eight categories, including the course overview and introduction, learning objectives, how outcomes are assessed and measured, the resources and materials used, activities that promote learner engagement, the technology in use and specifically whether the technology supports the stated learning objectives, the provision of links to learner support, and the accessibility of the course for disabled learners. Access to the Quality Matters Rubric and course evaluations based on the rubric occur through subscription.

If an institution is not connected to Quality Matters, how can an instructor determine if his or her course is effectively designed? Luckily, a growing body of literature is addressing this topic. Our own review of the literature (Palloff & Pratt, 2009) allowed us to establish the following categories of evaluation for an online course: student perception of the overall online course experience; orientation to the course and course materials; quantity and quality of material presented and the manner in which it is approached; activities that promote discussion and interaction student-to-student and student-to-instructor; learner self-assessment of participation and performance in the course, as well as the degree of contribution to the learning of others; ease of use of the course management system and its ability to support learning; access to technical support resources; and access to resources important to student learning. We return to these topics in more detail in Chapter Eight when we discuss the link between faculty and course evaluation and faculty development. Suffice it to say that design excellence will bring high marks in the outlined categories—learners seek clarity and variety in assignments (Chaney, Eddy, Dorman, Glessner, Green, & Lara-Alecio, 2007; Gaytan & McEwen, 2007), engagement both collectively and individually through discussion, reflection, and scholarly inquiry (Gunawardena, Ortegano-Layne, Carabajal, Frechette, Lindemann, & Jennings, 2006; Hawkes, 2006), relevant materials that align with the level of the learners in the course (Lynch & Dembo, 2004), a learning interface that supports interaction (Aycock, Garnham, & Kaleta, 2002; Beldarrain, 2006; Liao, 2006), and access to support (Chaney et al., 2007).

PROVIDING EFFECTIVE FACILITATION WHEN TEACHING COURSES DEVELOPED BY OTHERS

Not all instructors have the ability to design the courses they deliver. As institutions seek the ability to align course design with the growth of their online programs, the response is often to have one member of the faculty design a course that is delivered by many or that same faculty member may work with a course development team, again with the goal of creating a course that can be taught by any faculty member. In this case, effective facilitation and knowing how to adapt or modify a course written by another instructor are key indicators of excellence. An administrator we worked with noted that a good instructor can teach just about anything if he or she is well prepared. Thus, a well-trained online instructor should be able to effectively evaluate a course and determine how it should best be delivered.

The first question the instructor should ask in this situation is, How much can I customize this course? Customization should involve evaluation of what materials can and should be used or should be deleted, the addition of collaborative activities or additional discussion questions, and the ability to promote interactivity and create community. The goal should be to do all of this without sacrificing the learning objectives outlined in the course and staying true to the goals the course is attempting to achieve. We are both called upon to teach courses we did not write. Our first response is to modify by doing such things as creating banners to create visual appeal, adding discussion forums that promote community building, adding a blog site or a wiki assignment housed outside of the course management system, all in service of establishing presence, promoting collaboration, and creating community.

At times, institutions will ask instructors to teach a course exactly as it was written, limiting the ability to customize. In these cases, instructors still have the ability to enhance interactivity and increase access to content and course resources, if this is lacking, through the use of wikis, blogs, social networking sites, Internet search activities, and e-mail. One of the key criteria of instructor excellence is the ability to promote interaction. Consequently, every effort should be made to do so, whether it exists in the course or not.

GOOD FACILITATION ONLINE: WHAT IS INVOLVED?

Our emphasis, as we explore the topic of faculty excellence and faculty development, is on the importance of good facilitation skills. Skillful facilitation allows students to interact with one another and the instructor at a high level. Good facilitators monitor the discussion, asking probing questions to extend it, post announcements, and provide prompt feedback to students. Indicators that effective facilitation is occurring in an online course include the use of ice breaker activities at the start of the course and possibly at intervals throughout so that students can get to know one another and have fun doing so. A social space or café is included in the course and students are encouraged to use it. Clear participation expectations along with expectations for assignment completion are posted at the start of the course and students are invited to comment on them. In addition, discussion is a clear and regular part of the course and the instructor's input into that discussion is visible—asking questions to deepen the level of discourse and providing feedback on postings and assignments. Feedback is timely and timelines are explained at the start of the course. The instructor and other students offer additional information and content for students to explore and consider. The instructor may not act as the sole facilitator for the course—this responsibility may be shared with students; however, the instructor models good facilitation so as to promote these skills in learners.

Given the differences between face-to-face instruction and the facilitated approach that works best online, it is unrealistic to expect that instructors new to this form of education will simply know what to do. Skill in teaching online develops over time and with good training. What is the process a faculty member might go through in his or her development into an excellent online instructor? What forms of and approaches to faculty training are most likely to achieve success in this effort? Should faculty be encouraged to begin with hybrid instruction that combines face-to-face with online delivery and then gradually move to a fully online class? These are the questions we explore in Chapter Two. In addition, we explore the topic of faculty readiness to teach online—who should teach and how will we know if they are ready to take on this task?

KEY POINTS THAT DEFINE THE EXCELLENT ONLINE INSTRUCTOR

Based on our discussion thus far, some of the key elements that define excellence in online teaching are

- The excellent online instructor understands the differences between face-to-face and online teaching and can effectively implement them into development and facilitation of online classes.

- The excellent online instructor is committed to this form of teaching and uses the online environment to his or her advantage in delivering an online class.

- The excellent online instructor is able to establish presence early in the course and encourages students to do the same.

- The excellent online instructor is highly motivated and in turn is a good motivator for students.

- The excellent online instructor understands the importance of community building and devotes time at the start of the class to that function.

- The excellent online instructor promotes interactivity between students through development of good discussion questions that engage them and encourage them to seek out response material on their own.
- The excellent online instructor incorporates collaborative work into the design and delivery of an online class.
- The excellent online instructor respects students as partners in the learning process.
- The excellent online instructor is active and engaged throughout the course, providing timely, constructive feedback throughout.
- The excellent online instructor is open, flexible, compassionate, responsive, and leads by example.

This list might apply to any excellent instructor, whether teaching face-to-face or online. The main difference here is that the excellent *online* instructor accomplishes all of this through the use of technology and, in many cases, without ever meeting his or her students in person. The ability to accomplish all of this through the use of technology is what sets the excellent online instructor apart.

BECOMING YOUR OWN FACULTY DEVELOPER

Hara and Kling (2000) note that students need clear instruction for course expectations and assignments, reassurance that their ideas are on track, a reasonable load in terms of the amount of reading, posting, and elements such as e-mail, prompt and unambiguous feedback, and technical support. The Illinois Online Network (2007) provides a list of what the participants of the online experience can expect from the facilitator–instructor. This list includes creating assignments that incorporate students' life and educational experiences, that easily allow the student to translate theory into practice, and that involve minimal to no lecturing.

Developing ability or skill in an area involves taking an inventory of the skills you possess first so that you know the areas on which you need to focus. As you begin your journey toward excellence, think about, complete, and respond to the following self-assessment tasks and questions:

- Write an introductory letter to your students that describes who you are, how you teach or facilitate, and what you expect from your learners. Give that letter to your students and ask for feedback—what questions did it leave unanswered? How can it be improved?

- Assess your own ability to establish presence and create community in your online course. How do you accomplish this currently? How might you change or improve your approach?

- Focus on one unit of your online course—how can you increase interactivity in that unit? How might you redesign it in order to empower learners to take on the bulk of responsibility for the learning process? How might you assess the learning outcomes without the use of a test or quiz?

- How often are you currently logging into your online course? How often do you think you should log in? Does your class need more attention from you?

- How many of the characteristics of the excellent online instructor do you currently possess? How might you make progress in developing the characteristics you might not have?

Phases of Development

Cravener (1998) reports on an e-mail discussion with a graduate student describing the student's less-than-satisfying experiences in online classes. The graduate student wrote that "throughout her three years of distance courses from an accredited university, professors made it abundantly clear that they knew little about the technology, did not wish to spend time with the technology, and preferred not to teach at a distance if at all possible" (p. 1). Although we would love to say that this has changed dramatically over the last decade or so, we know that there are still many professors who feel this way. A recent phone conversation with an administrator at a university that has been delivering classes in hybrid fashion revealed that his faculty would rather have a root canal than engage in threaded discussion in the online component of their classes! Given that we consider threaded discussion to be the heart of an online course, this comment is an indicator that misunderstanding continues to exist about how online learning is best conducted and that the need for training persists in order to achieve excellence online.

Excellent online instructors rarely emerge "out of the box" but develop their skills over time. Benor (n.d.) presents a phased approach to faculty development for new instructors, beginning with orientation to the university, then moving to training in basic instructional skills, specific instructional skills pertinent to the instructor's discipline, and finally the development of educational leadership. He further describes faculty development as a process of personal growth that involves repetitive exposure to education as a discipline, the incorporation of feedback from real-life experience in training experiences, and self-selection of topics and areas of interest for ongoing development. Faculty involvement in choosing what they need to learn in faculty development efforts is echoed by several authors exploring this topic (POD Network, 2007; Cravener, 1998; Travis, 1995–96). The POD (Professional and Organizational Development) Network (2007) notes that faculty development programs focus on the faculty member as a teacher, the faculty member as a scholar and professional, and the faculty member as a person. They note that the direction of the program should be determined by the faculty and supported by administration. Our experience in faculty development for online teaching is that the impetus for such programs comes from many sources—the teaching and learning centers on campus, administrators interested in expanding course offerings in the online arena, and faculty themselves who want to become more skilled at working online. Like the classroom instructor, the online instructor needs a training approach that addresses where he or she is in the process of developing skills for online teaching—one size does not fit all.

The phases of the "emergence" of a good online instructor along with his or her training needs will be explored in this chapter along with what is needed to support that development. This chapter also addresses faculty readiness to teach online and a model of phased faculty development for online teaching that includes

- Developing and establishing presence
- The incorporation of classroom experiences and student feedback into faculty development
- The use of mentors and champions
- Advanced development—the development of lifelong learners

FACULTY READINESS TO TEACH ONLINE

Like students, faculty are sometimes drawn to the online teaching because of its convenience—both faculty and students can engage in online learning at any hour of the day or night. Some faculty are drawn to online teaching because it clearly is the latest trend in teaching and they want to stay employable and on top of new developments. Still others are simply assigned to teach online and are given no choice in the matter. Many faculty have little to no idea about what is involved with online teaching, seeing it as no different from what goes on in the face-to-face classroom and, once they begin, experience what Mezirow (1990) terms a "disorienting dilemma" as they enter an environment that is alien to them. In the online classroom, they find that their disciplinary expertise and reliance on what they have always done as an instructor is not what they can rely on to assist them in making the transition. One of us recently received a phone call from a new graduate from a doctoral program who had been applying to numerous universities in order to get a job teaching online and was frustrated that she was not being considered. As the conversation progressed, it became evident that she had never taken an online class and had no idea about what happens in one. She could not understand how an instructor could be based in California and work with students in New York, given the time differences. Cleary, the realities of online teaching were disorienting to her and she could not figure out how to present herself in the face of that disorientation so as to get hired. She was advised to first research what online teaching was all about and possibly even take an online class before continuing her job search so that she would be better able to present herself to potential employers and demonstrate understanding of what she was hoping to do. This example demonstrates one of the issues faced by novice online faculty: they don't even know what questions to ask as they begin.

How do we know if someone is ready to enter online teaching? What does it take to at least get started in the field? Just as online quizzes exist in various locations on the Internet for potential online students to self-assess their potential success with online classes, so do such self-assessments exist for faculty. Penn State University and Central Florida University (2008) collaborated to develop a comprehensive self-assessment that allows faculty to explore their skills and abilities in four categories: organization and time management, communication skills online, teaching and online experience, and technical skills. Once the assessment is completed, the potential instructor receives a report both online and via e-mail that provides feedback on responses, along with information in each category to support the feedback and offer advice for development. The assessment focuses on planning and organization and also looks at the new or potential instructor's experience and comfort with various forms of technology, including course management systems, word processing, and social networking technology. There is one question devoted to the ability to develop presence online, but there are no questions that assess the potential faculty member's ability to adjust his or her teaching style to what is demanded when teaching online. In other words, what is the faculty member's orientation to active, collaborative learning and how does he or she view the creation of a learning community in the delivery of online courses? We offer our own version of such a self-assessment in Appendix A: Resources for Faculty Developers and Those Tasked with Faculty Development.

Assessment of faculty readiness to teach online should be based on the criteria for excellence in online instruction that we began discussing in Chapter One. To reiterate, the criteria for the excellent online instructor include

- *Visibility*—the excellent online instructor can establish presence and *is* present frequently in the online environment.
- *Compassion*—defined by openness, concern, flexibility, fairness, and honesty—the excellent online instructor expresses sincere positive regard for students and delivers student-focused, student-centered instruction.
- *Communication*—the excellent online instructor communicates with students frequently, provides substantive feedback, and communicates well using technology.
- *Commitment*—the excellent online instructor is not only a passionate and committed teacher, but sees the value in teaching online and sees the facilitated model of teaching as rigorous and powerful. The excellent online instructor is motivated and a good motivator.
- *Organization*—the excellent online instructor is organized and a good time-manager.

What is assumed is that the excellent online instructor is an expert in his or her discipline. This is not necessarily a prerequisite for excellent online teaching, as we assume that all faculty are hired to teach because of their disciplinary expertise. The excellent online instructor understands, however, that the context for the use of technology in teaching is the discipline; in other words, they are able to make the connections between the learning outcomes they seek and the use of technology to achieve them, using those technologies as a vehicle for student achievement. As we mentioned earlier, faculty do not achieve excellence online in their first course. With this as a backdrop, we now turn to a discussion of what is involved in moving faculty toward excellence.

THE PHASES OF ONLINE FACULTY DEVELOPMENT

Our experience in conducting faculty development for online teaching spans well over a decade and has demonstrated to us that faculty do indeed go through phases of development. We have identified five distinct phases, which we have called

- *Visitor*—those faculty who have toyed with the idea of technology integration in their face-to-face classes and who may have posted a syllabus or assignments online or used e-mail for assignment completion.

- *Novice*—those faculty who have never taught online and who may or may not have taken an online course as a student but have consistently posted a syllabus online and have used some communications technologies to supplement their face-to-face teaching.

- *Apprentice*—those faculty who have taught online for one or two terms. They may have taught more than one course per term. They are developing an understanding of the online environment and the skills required to teach online.

- *Insider*—those faculty who have taught more than two semesters online and have taught more than one course per term. They feel comfortable in the online environment, are proficient with course management technology, and have basic understanding of the skills needed for online teaching. They may have designed one or more online courses.

- *Master*—those faculty who have taught online for multiple terms and have designed several online courses. They have mastered the technology required to teach online and are likely to have integrated technology beyond the course management system into their teaching. They feel extremely comfortable with the skills required to teach online and can be called upon for peer support for newer online faculty.

Clearly, these phases are not finite—some faculty who might be considered apprentices or even insiders may view themselves as novices depending on how well they are coming to understand what is required of them online. Consequently, faculty at each stage of development may have very different training needs. However, there are four categories of need that we believe are present in each phase and that go beyond the focus on time management and the use of technology, which are the topics often stressed in faculty development programs in many colleges and universities. They are

- *Personal*—focusing on the instructor as a person and including such elements as establishing presence and developing confidence in one's ability to teach online
- *Pedagogy*—focusing on the skills and techniques involved with teaching online and on online scholarship, including an understanding of the theories that undergird online teaching and the ability to develop an online learning community.
- *Content*—focusing on the discipline the faculty member represents and how that content is best disseminated online.
- *Technology*—focusing on the development of skill with the course management system in use, choosing technologies that meet learning objectives, as well as adjunct technologies that might be incorporated into the development of an online course as well as teaching.

The categories of need do not necessarily hold equal weight through the developmental phases. For example, novice faculty members are likely to have stronger needs in the personal and pedagogical areas. Their needs in the technology area would probably be focused on simply getting the course management system to work for them in the delivery of their courses, but would not be focused on developing high-level technological skill. Content would also probably take a back seat to simply figuring out what to do the first time through. In contrast, elder or master faculty would be more focused on developing higher-level technological skills and advancing the scholarship of online teaching. Figure 2.1 is a graphic representation of the model. The model is cyclical in nature not to represent that faculty start the process over again, but to indicate that master faculty become trainers and mentors of faculty in the cycle once they reach that level. Also, the listing of the elements within each category differs depending on their importance to that group of faculty. The elements within each category are listed with the most important on the top of the list, moving to the least important element in that category.

We now look at each phase and its connection to the four categories depicted in the model.

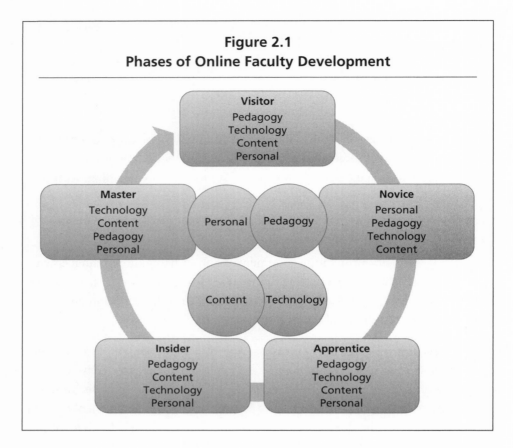

Figure 2.1
Phases of Online Faculty Development

Visitor
Pedagogy
Technology
Content
Personal

Master
Technology
Content
Pedagogy
Personal

Personal

Pedagogy

Novice
Personal
Pedagogy
Technology
Content

Content

Technology

Insider
Pedagogy
Content
Technology
Personal

Apprentice
Pedagogy
Technology
Content
Personal

Visitor

Visitors to online teaching are curious about what's possible, but may avoid full commitment to teaching online due to concerns about time and their knowledge of technology. Therefore, they tend to use those elements of course management systems or communication technologies with which they feel comfortable. Often this amounts to posting a syllabus online or by attachment to an e-mail and using e-mail to communicate with students. Rarely does the visitor go beyond this point in a term or in a class and may not consistently use these technologies, preferring to communicate with students face-to-face. They may be skeptical and may need a bit of convincing to move forward. They will often ask questions that include these: What is the point of teaching online? How will it benefit my students and me? How can I justify the time it takes to teach online? Isn't face-to-face teaching more rigorous and effective?

Visitors may or may not attend seminars offered by their college or university about technology integration unless they cover topics of interest to them. Because they are dipping their toes into virtual water, they might be better impacted by individual or small group sessions at the department level or demonstrations of the use of technology that clearly link its use to learning outcomes (Zhu, 2008). Teclehaimanot and Lamb (2005) described a three-year faculty development program for the integration of technology into teaching. They began with a survey where faculty were asked what they wanted to learn and workshops were developed around those topics, many of which did not apply to online teaching (such as the use of PowerPoint) but nevertheless attracted a significant number of faculty. Beginning by helping visitors explore the technology they might use in their face-to-face classes helps break down barriers to technology use in general and begins to warm faculty to the idea of teaching online. Instead of seeing technology as a necessary evil, visitors may begin to see the useful impact of technology as a time-saver, as well as a means by which to increase achievement of student learning outcomes.

Training needs for visitors include

- *Personal:* Break down skepticism and demonstrate that technology use can enhance student learning; provide examples and models; personalize training by providing workshops, seminars, and individual instruction in topics of interest to this group.

- *Pedagogy:* Show direct links between technology use and learning outcomes through models and examples, as well as through review of syllabi, to determine appropriate use of technology within face-to-face instruction and online means.

- *Content:* Demonstrate use of technology within the discipline, that is, how can media-rich presentations enhance instruction in math, biology, languages, history, and so forth?

- *Technology:* Focus only on technology that might enhance face-to-face instruction and addresses learning objectives as a start while increasing familiarity with online options.

Novice

Novice faculty are more than curious about teaching online and really want to try to move beyond the visitor stage but often enter the world of online teaching with some anxiety and fear. They are likely to be unsure about how to set up a class, as well as how to deliver it. They may have heard horror stories about how long it actually takes to teach online and may worry about their ability to manage their time, connect with students they cannot see or hear, convey content from their disciplines, and assess student work. As previously mentioned, they often don't even know what questions to ask in order to get started. Questions that we often hear from novice faculty, however, include, How do I lecture online? How do I know that the student is doing his or her own work? What do I do about cheating? How do I teach using the course management system (CMS)? Although these questions are shared to some extent by more experienced online faculty, novice faculty experience them as a source of fear of the unknown rather than concern about skill development. As a result, many novice faculty may use the CMS in minimal ways by posting a syllabus and assignments but making little to no use of the discussion boards and other communication tools contained therein, although these are likely to be the most important tools for online teaching. Zhu (2008) notes that this problem is compounded by the ways in which technology training occurs. Training often happens in large campuswide seminars that are not conducted based on level of skill and are rarely tied to disciplinary teaching or learning outcomes. Zhu further notes that faculty will sometimes attend these sessions with no anticipation that the skills taught will be relevant to their teaching. Our experience in delivering training on numerous campuses supports this observation—we often have faculty participating who are curious about online learning but have no plans to teach online or to integrate technology into their face-to-face teaching.

Novice faculty, in particular, benefit from beginning training experiences as a learner and then transitioning to the instructor role by preparing and presenting material to peers within the training experience and receiving feedback for improvement. By providing a safe space for experimentation and receipt of feedback, novice faculty can gain confidence in their ability to transition to the online environment. This approach helps them to learn ways in which to deliver content without lecturing and how to facilitate a discussion more effectively. It is appropriate to reassure novice faculty that using basic "read and discuss" techniques for their first class is a good place to start; this helps reduce the fear that they will make mistakes in facilitation and encourages them to gain experience with elements of the CMS that go beyond the posting of a syllabus and assignments. Consequently, training needs to focus on the use of the discussion board and ways in which to construct assignments and assess student learning.

These faculty need to understand that adding additional collaborative activities and adjunct technologies can wait until they feel more confident and have the experience of having taught a course or two.

Training needs for novice faculty include

- *Personal:* Reassure and help overcome any fears about online teaching; help gain confidence through training experiences that provide a transition from learner to instructor; assist with establishing presence online; explore personal teaching style and support any transitions needed for good online teaching.

- *Pedagogy:* Explore the theoretical underpinnings of online teaching and learning; explore beginning techniques to support best practices in online teaching; support and critique the development of the instructor's first online course; help them to surface the questions they need to ask in order to begin teaching online; offer ongoing support through training and mentoring as they embark on their first course experience.

- *Content:* Explore appropriate teaching techniques for the discipline; support alternatives to traditional teaching methods in the discipline so as to develop techniques other than lecture for delivering content.

- *Technology:* Gain mastery of the course management system (CMS) in use; master appropriate use of e-mail and chat; support the development of the use of word processing and presentation technologies such as Word and PowerPoint; introduce the use of authoring tools for course and lesson development.

Apprentice

Faculty who have one or two terms of online teaching experience are likely to have overcome the initial fears about the environment and how to connect with students but may be encountering new fears as they begin to understand what they don't know about teaching online. Their concerns at this juncture involve moving to the next level; in other words, Now that I know how to navigate and facilitate an online course at a basic level, how can I improve my skills to increase learner participation and incorporate teaching techniques beyond "read and discuss?" Often the questions we get from this group of faculty focus on establishing presence and improving facilitation skills: How can I let my students know who I am beyond my CV? How can I increase the level of participation in my class? How do I get students to talk to one another? How can I use the CMS more effectively? Beginning faculty benefit from a training environment where they are able to share experiences resulting from their online teaching and receive feedback and suggestions from peers. It helps them to know that they are not alone in experiencing some of the challenges and also in sharing the successes of teaching online. Training needs, then, involve a reinforcement of what they are doing well along with suggestions to take things to the next level in their classes by adding more collaborative or small-group activity, for example, or adding technologies to promote collaboration, such as the use of wikis and blogs.

Training needs for apprentice faculty include

- *Personal:* Continue to gain confidence by reviewing and reinforcing online teaching experiences; continue to reinforce a sense of presence online; reassure by surfacing and addressing questions and concerns and reinforce successes.
- *Pedagogy:* Use course and student feedback for course and facilitation improvement; focus on the integration of collaborative teaching and skills to build an online learning community; continue to explore theoretical foundations of online teaching.
- *Content:* Content concerns are greater at this phase of development and added focus on alternative techniques for facilitating content exploration is important; encourage involvement in communities of practice centered around the discipline.
- *Technology:* Begin the exploration of adjunct technologies to support course development, collaboration, and to increase student participation, such as beginning use of wikis, blogs, synchronous technologies, and social networking technologies; continue to develop skill in the use of authoring tools.

Insider

Insider faculty, or faculty who have taught a number of online courses for several terms, have the need of reviewing and reinforcing skills while also moving forward toward more advanced skill development. Advanced skill development includes the use of adjunct media in the design and delivery of a course, reliance on collaborative methods in online teaching, and engagement with more advanced assessment techniques, including application activities, collaborative assessment, and the like. Insider faculty have developed more confidence in the delivery of materials in their content areas but continue to benefit from participation in communities of practice to support that work. Training needs, however, may be more discipline-specific rather than focused on general skills for online teaching. Questions we often hear from this group of faculty include, How can I assess student work without the use of tests and quizzes? How can I use a learning community approach in math (or science, or accounting, etc.)? How can I help my students take on more responsibility for their learning?

Training needs for insider faculty include

- *Personal:* Continued reinforcement of presence; support of growing confidence in online teaching abilities.
- *Pedagogy:* Support for techniques in the development of an online learning community; techniques for empowering learners; exploration of more advanced topics in online teaching, including collaborative means of content delivery.
- *Content:* Continue to support participation with those in the discipline to explore best practices in delivering content online.
- *Technology:* Advanced training in adjunct technologies to support course development and facilitation, such as course authoring tools, wikis, blogs, synchronous media, and social networking tools.

Master

Like elders in a community who hold significant wisdom, master faculty are those who have a great deal of experience with online teaching and who are willing to experiment with new techniques for course development and delivery. Often they can be called upon to support the development of their colleagues who are at earlier stages in the process and should be supported in doing so through mentoring programs or as peer trainers. They also support the discipline of online teaching by conducting research, presenting at conferences, and publishing their work, which may include both the results of their research and the results of practice. Master faculty continue to have questions about best practices and are in need of training to support advanced skill development.

Training needs for master faculty include

- *Personal:* Support for leadership development and expertise in online teaching; presentation to their peers and at conferences; support for publication.
- *Pedagogy:* Support for exploration and study of advanced facilitation techniques; encourage development for peer training.

- *Content:* Support continued exploration of best practices for online teaching within the discipline and encourage research into the outcomes of such practices.
- *Technology:* Support for development and inclusion of new technologies and new approaches in the use of technology in online teaching.

THE KEY TO UNDERSTANDING THE PHASES

What is key to working with a phased approach to online faculty development is the recognition that faculty enter the training process at different places in their development. A mistake that many institutions make is assuming that someone new to the institution is also new to online teaching. If someone has been teaching online at another institution, insisting that they complete training in basic skills for online teaching is a waste of time for both the new faculty member and the institution. Online experience needs to be honored and respected with training experiences matched to the levels of experience we have described. Zhu (2008) notes that the majority of faculty who attend workshops on integrating technology into teaching are not necessarily risk-takers and self-starters. Instead, they need instruction on how to use technology to maximize learning outcomes—in other words, how to tie technology to teaching and learning. Training on the "how to's" of a software package often do not meet this goal and may leave faculty more frustrated. As a result, Zhu recommends the use of decentralized support on large campuses. This is accomplished by integrating a combination of the support offered through the centralized office charged with supporting technology integration and the use of hardware/software support personnel at the department level. He recommends a collaborative approach, developing a community of support for faculty.

Although some larger institutions may have a number of people who have been hired for the purpose of supporting the use of technology in teaching and are more likely to have a center devoted to teaching and learning, smaller campuses often do not have this available to them. Mooney and Reder (2008) discuss the difficulty of delivering faculty development programs on small campuses, noting that often faculty developers are pulled from the ranks of faculty, rarely have any support staff, and find themselves in a situation of wearing too many hats. Time constraints are critical and can sink a faculty development effort on any campus large or small. Sustainability becomes another critical issue on small campuses—budget strains often impact the delivery of such services. Consequently, making use of experienced or master faculty to support training and development needs, model best practices, act as a resource for colleagues, and act as mentors can meet these needs at lower cost. Mooney and Reder discuss the common elements of faculty development programs on small campuses, which include faculty participation is voluntary; faculty were asked to commit to a series of meetings with a community of colleagues, even if the topics changed; regular meeting times and common readings were established; and faculty were asked to reflect on and discuss their experiences in the faculty development program. These common elements reflect the principle with which we began this chapter—faculty need to be involved in determining what they learn and how they learn it. Another approach to doing so is the use of mentoring programs.

FACULTY MENTORING FOR ONLINE TEACHING

Although we will devote significantly more discussion to the topic of mentoring and offer examples of mentoring programs for online teaching in Chapter Six, some discussion of mentoring is warranted here. Many institutions formally or informally assign more experienced online faculty to mentor or coach new faculty as they design or deliver, or both, their first online classes. This is not done as part of administrative evaluation of faculty, but as a way to ensure quality, improve performance over time, answer immediate questions as they arise, and provide new online faculty members with someone they can access quickly as problems and concerns emerge.

Boice (1992), a noted author and researcher on mentoring, describes the benefits of faculty mentoring as the support of professional growth and renewal. Boice (2000) states that many faculty believe that spontaneous mentoring is the most successful. However, he cautions that due to time constraints, spontaneous mentoring relationships rarely last, thus giving credence to the need for a more formal, structured mentoring program. Gray and Birch (2008) provide evidence to support a group mentoring approach through their discussions of some of the failures of mentoring programs: often, when faculty are simply matched as mentor (senior faculty member) and mentee (new faculty member) without choice, the mentoring relationship is structured as a top-down relationship that may struggle and fail. This can be the unfortunate outcome of what is referred to as "traditional mentoring" (Yun & Sorcinelli, 2009).

The group approach to mentoring, as described by Gray and Birch, or the "networked" approach as described by Yun and Sorcinelli (2009), supports our own notion of using a community of practice, or a faculty learning community, as a means by which to help faculty effectively transition to the online environment. Critical to the success of such a learning community is the inclusion of faculty at all phases of development for online learning. Group mentoring or a collaborative community-oriented approach can take the form of regularly scheduled brown-bag lunches where topics related to online learning are presented and discussed, group seminars and conferences, and even group research on various aspects of online learning. By working within a learning community focused on online learning, faculty members can experience the benefits of online work and can then translate those into their online teaching. We explore specific means by which such mentoring programs can be developed and implemented in Chapter Six. Suffice it to say at this point that the use of a community approach helps meet the individual training needs of faculty at all phases of development while promoting best practices in online teaching.

DEALING WITH FACULTY RESISTANCE

What should be clear at this point is that forcing faculty to teach online or to engage in faculty development activities for that purpose may, and often does, meet with significant resistance. This is particularly true for faculty who are assigned to teach online but who have not expressed interest in doing so. In essence, these faculty members have been "forced" to teach online. A recent consulting and training experience illustrates how resistance can manifest when faculty are pushed to teach online whether they want to or not. We were hired by a large, public institution that had an initiative to move a significant amount of instruction online—the institution could no longer invest in building new classrooms and saw their growth potential in offering online classes. In addition, their accrediting organization felt that the training they were offering faculty prior to teaching online was insufficient. They applied for and received some grant money to train as many faculty as they could in a short period and offered a stipend to any faculty member who chose to attend and participate in the training. They further announced that anyone who either was teaching or planned to teach online must complete the training. Although we warned the administrators that this was not a good approach and could create problems for them, well over

70 faculty signed up for the training—many of whom were more interested in receiving the stipend than teaching online and many of whom would not be teaching online in the near future. The result? We experienced significant resistance to our ideas and suggestions. Faculty members in the group were vocal about their disagreement with us and were disrespectful and resistant throughout. Our attempts to engage more experienced faculty to assist the less experienced provided a bit of success in this difficult situation—as much as we could, we had them work in discipline-specific small groups where the more experienced could help the novices begin the development of their online courses. Overall, this was an extremely frustrating experience for us but did illustrate that the resistance could be managed to some degree.

On many campuses, administrators have determined (often with good reason) that it is imperative to move instruction online in order to attract and retain students. Clay (1999) attributes resistance to online teaching to a number of factors and offers the following strategies for overcoming them:

- *Increased workload*—Set reasonable class size limits (we recommend 20 to 25 students in an online class) and allow release time or reimbursement for course development.

- *Altered role of the instructor*—Assist with paradigm shift from teaching to learning and base course designs on sound learning principles (we discuss how this can be done in the next chapter on training strategies and techniques).

- *Lack of technical and administrative support*—Provide adequate software training and technical support and set up a Help Desk for both faculty and students.

- *Perceived reduction in course quality*—Determine sound educational theory and principles to support course development; integrate online learning into program evaluation and outcomes assessment.

- *Negative attitudes of other faculty*—Support innovators to serve as role models and reward innovation; support voluntary participation.

We offer some additional suggestions for overcoming resistance:

- *Use attraction as a means of recruitment*—Although they are smaller in number on many campuses, there are "first wave" faculty (Zhu, 2008) who will readily attend workshops and seminars on various forms of technology and on integrating technology into their teaching. These faculty members can be used as champions of the process, talking to their colleagues about their successes and what they are learning as they transition their work online. We can't stress enough, as Clay (1999) did, that making participation in online teaching voluntary to start with is a far superior strategy to demanding that faculty teach online.

- *Be satisfied with whatever numbers attend*—Gray and Birch (2008) note that on smaller campuses, where most faculty know one another, attendance at a seminar by even a few faculty can have a multiplier effect. Those faculty will take what they learned back to their colleagues; those who resisted attending may find that they missed a good training opportunity and may be more inclined to attend the next time around. The voluntary nature of the training helps reduce resistance.

- *Include faculty in initial training sessions who are ready to teach*—We have been asked on many occasions to offer general training to as many faculty who are interested in online teaching. When that training is offered online, resistance emerges from those who cannot or who will not be putting that training to immediate use. As interest grows and online teaching opportunities increase on campus, broader inclusion makes sense. But to begin with, only include those faculty who will be making immediate use of the training in initial sessions devoted to online teaching, learning the course management system, and so forth.

- *Individualize training*—If frustration emerges from those who are moving more slowly or those who are moving more rapidly, develop just-in-time mentoring relationships within the training situation and provide extra support to those who are struggling.

- *Create training experiences that are fun*—Nothing helps more to increase levels of resistance than training experiences that are deadly boring and seen as a waste of time. Link training to student learning outcomes and include games, food, and other means to engage the audience. We discuss this further in the next chapter when we focus on training techniques.

In general, we have found that resistance emerges from fear of the unknown—fear in this case may be fear of the technology or the fear that the lack of expertise may expose faculty in ways that will be an embarrassment to them. Consequently, it is important to be sensitive to these issues and not see resistance as something to be overcome, but rather something to be worked with. In the next chapter, we focus on specific training techniques for online faculty. The development and delivery of good training experiences, based on adult learning theory, can also help reduce resistance while improving the practice of online teaching, thus moving faculty toward excellence.

KEY POINTS REGARDING TRAINING NEEDS AND PHASES OF DEVELOPMENT FOR THE EXCELLENT ONLINE INSTRUCTOR

In this chapter, we examined a phased model of development for online teaching along with the needs faculty bring to the development process. Some of the key points related to development and training needs are

- Faculty experience differing needs at various points in their development. Focusing only on time management skills and the use of technology misses the most important of these needs—how the instructor defines himself or herself and establishes presence in the online environment.

- The key is paying attention to the instructor as a person and developing training experiences that begin with and are responsive to where that faculty member happens to be in the process.

- A community-oriented, collaborative approach exposes faculty to multiple perspectives and provides a broad base of support in the development process. Group mentoring for online teaching is likely to be superior to one-to-one mentoring as a result.

- It is important to avoid direct confrontation of faculty resistance to online teaching itself as well as training for online teaching by using champions to help them work through the fear—again, it is the "person" aspect of development that is most critical in order to make the transition to online work most effective.

- Make it fun! Convey the excitement that can be part of online learning through the use of games and other activities that engage the audience and get them laughing.

BECOMING YOUR OWN FACULTY DEVELOPER

In the last chapter, we asked you to engage in a self-assessment to look at your teaching skills and abilities and how those may or may not translate to the online environment. Now we'd like you to look specifically at the demands of the online environment itself and determine if you're ready to move forward. To do so

- Go to Appendix B and complete the Assessment of Faculty Readiness to Teach Online.

- How did you do on the self-assessment? Are you ready? What do you need to do to get ready if you are not?

- Where do you see yourself in the development model we presented in this chapter and what training needs do you think you have?

- Based on your responses to the previous questions, begin to develop a training and action plan for yourself. Included in Appendix A is an Individual Training Plan that you can use to help you build an action plan for self-development. Make sure to include the resources available to you or those you will need to seek out as you implement your plan. Also, make sure to include a timeline and stick to it!

chapter THREE

Elements of Training for Excellence

Faculty development works. It assists faculty in making changes in their beliefs and attitudes about learning, approach to teaching and learning, as well as the techniques involved with teaching and learning (Barlett & Rappoport, 2009; Hewson, Copeland, & Fishleder, 2000; Stern, 2003; Sweet, Roberts, Walker, and others, 2008). Although faculty development for online teaching also must be concerned about and focused on attitudes, beliefs, and techniques, it has the added element of the use of technology for teaching and learning. Moore, Moore, and Fowler (2009) note that expertise for online teaching needs to go beyond how to use technology in pedagogical practice. What must be included is an understanding of how our students learn by means of technology and how they perceive the use of technology in their online classes and their lives. Consequently, not only do potential online instructors need to examine their own attitudes and beliefs about the inclusion of technology in teaching, they also should be aware of their students' needs where technology is concerned and how they are using technology outside of the classroom.

With this as a backdrop, in this chapter we examine approaches to developing good faculty training along with the theoretical and technological basis for training. Included in this discussion is a multipronged approach to training and development that incorporates adult learning theory, the use of technology, and research on effective strategies for online faculty development. Other considerations are the optimum length of training, who should develop and deliver training, and an exploration of the benefits of online versus face-to-face training versus a hybrid approach.

WHAT DOES GOOD FACULTY TRAINING LOOK LIKE?

Caffarella (2002) summarizes the major principles of adult learning theory that should be taken into account when planning training for faculty:

- Adults learn best when their experience is acknowledged and new knowledge is built on past knowledge and experience.
- Adults are both intrinsically and extrinsically motivated to learn.
- All adults have preferred ways of learning and processing information.
- Adults are not likely to participate in learning situations unless they are meaningful to them.
- Adults are pragmatic in their learning and want to directly apply what they are learning.
- Adults come to learning situations with personal goals and objectives that may not align with the planned goals and objectives.
- Adults prefer to be active rather than passive learners.
- Adults learn using collaborative and interdependent means, as well as independently.
- Adults are more receptive to learning when it occurs in environments that are physically and psychologically comfortable for them.

Let's now look at each of these as they impact faculty training for online teaching and learning. In so doing, we have combined some of the principles that relate to one another, thus expanding the concept in practice.

Adults learn best when their experience is acknowledged and new knowledge is built on past knowledge and experience. As we presented in Chapter Two, faculty development for online teaching is a phased process—not all faculty enter this process at the same place or progress at the same rate. In addition, as we discussed, their training needs vary by phase. This said, novice faculty come into the process with little to no online experience but are likely to have potentially significant experience with "on the ground" teaching. They are also likely to have significant experience within their disciplines. At the other end of the continuum, master faculty are likely to have significant online experience, as well as significant teaching and disciplinary experience. However, in our experience, many institutions continue to deliver one-size-fits-all programs, which do not address the developmental phase in which faculty find themselves. If an insider or master faculty happens to change institutional affiliation, often he or she is forced to go through apprentice training for online teaching, something that is a waste of time and money, often leading to frustration. Hagner (2001) states, "Administrators must realize that faculty vary considerably in both their abilities and attitudes toward the new technologies and that institutional-based attempts to engage the faculty must take these variations into account in order to be successful" (p. 2). Although all faculty need orientation to the policies and procedures of a new institution, not all faculty need the same level of technological and pedagogical training.

It is important to remember that online teaching presents a disorienting dilemma to many faculty (Mezirow, 1990). Given that adults prefer to build new knowledge on past experience, a lack of experience in this area can pose significant challenges and frustrations. This needs to be acknowledged and supported. Trainers of novice faculty need to approach the training with a beginner's mind, remembering what their own first online experiences were like and pacing the training to coincide with the rhythm of mastery. In other words, trainers cannot rigidly adhere to a training schedule that will leave some faculty behind while others are impatient to move forward. Zhu (2008) recommends that flexible training schedules be developed and Hagner (2001) further recommends the development of a comprehensive, integrated package of training approaches coupled with support. As we discuss later in the chapter, models that incorporate face-to-face and online training along with solid support through mentoring, technical support, and the development of a faculty learning community can result in what Hagner terms "best systems" (p. 31) for developing excellent faculty and an equally excellent online program.

Adults are both intrinsically and extrinsically motivated to learn. Hagner (2001) presents four categories of faculty and their motivation to engage in faculty training for online learning and the use of technology itself. The "entrepreneurs," also known as the "first wave" faculty, are those who are interested in technology integration simply because they possess some expertise and are interested in bettering the teaching and learning process through its use. Their motivation to do so is internal and the usual incentives offered by academic institutions for technology integration are not motivators for them. "Second-wave" faculty share the first-wave faculty's interest in advancing education through technology but are less experienced and more risk-averse. Not looking for an incentive to integrate technology, this group is more concerned with the amount of effort it takes to do so and need significant support. The provision of that support is their motivator to continue. "Careerist" faculty are the third type. These faculty are interested in advancing their careers in the academy and see the adoption of technology as a way of doing so. The careerist is motivated by university incentives and reward structures. Finally, the "reluctants" are the faculty who resist the integration of technology into teaching. They have an "if it ain't broke, why fix it?" mentality, insisting that face-to-face instruction is far superior to that delivered via technology. Some of the faculty we have called "visitors" are likely to fall into this category as well. As their colleagues begin to utilize technology, and as their students begin to demand it, the reluctants experience significant pressure to get on board or suffer potential career disadvantages. Often it is other faculty who can motivate the reluctant to try the use of technology; administrative pressure is not likely to be successful.

Hagner's categories demonstrate that one incentive will not fit all when it comes to technology integration. Just as training needs to be individualized, so do incentives so that the first-wave faculty are supported in continuing their work online while the reluctants and visitors are gradually coming to the party.

Adults are not likely to participate in learning situations unless they are meaningful to them and adults are pragmatic in their learning and want to directly apply what they are learning. As we discussed in Chapter Two, it is important to train faculty for online teaching when they are most ready to participate—in other words, when faculty are ready to start teaching online, then training should occur. Robinson (2003) states that when new technologies are introduced on campus, successful implementation of them is dependent on "the technology being used by the right people, at the right time, with the right methods" (p. 34). Timing of technology integration and timing of training are critical. Given that Zhu (2008) notes that faculty have difficulty connecting technology training to learning outcomes, particularly within their disciplines, giving faculty the opportunity to learn something, practice it, and then return for feedback helps create those connections. When faculty are unable to engage in this cycle of learn, do, reflect, in our experience they have difficulty making meaning of what they have learned and will often become frustrated. Because we don't want to set faculty up to fail, conducting training online prior to embarking on their first online course experience can help faculty engage in the cycle of learn, do, and reflect with their peers. We devote much more attention to the benefits of online training for online teaching later in this chapter.

Also, the time during the academic year that training is offered will determine who will be able to participate and then make use of the training. Zhu states that in the experience of his institution, training carried out in May attracted more people who were willing to not only attend but also implement what they learned. Surveying faculty to determine timing of training, then, is a factor that may influence the success of an online learning effort.

Adults come to learning situations with personal goals and objectives that may not align with the planned goals and objectives. Barker (2003) and the POD Network (n.d.) both note the importance of gaining faculty buy-in for any faculty development program. Barker states that it is important to engage faculty in goal setting for training for online teaching. What assists in this process is helping faculty see the benefits of online teaching. Included are such factors as the ability to place the responsibility for learning squarely on students, the ability to develop rich discussions related to content using the discussion board, and the development and use of new forms of communication with students. According to Caffarella (2002), training programs must be able to answer the question "Why are we doing this?" in order to effectively engage participants.

Critical to the start of any training experience is surveying the participants to determine what they hope to get from that training while sharing the goals and objectives for the training as determined by the planners and trainers. If possible, training should be tailored to the desired outcomes of the participants and yet meet program objectives. Caffarella warns against developing training program outcomes and objectives in a vacuum. Involving faculty in the design and development of the training that will be delivered can help to ensure that the voice of the participants is heard and that training is relevant to faculty needs.

Adults prefer to be active rather than passive learners and learn via collaborative and interdependent means and independently. The means by which training is conducted is perhaps more critical than the content of the training itself. One of us was invited to attend a training session at a local university where Blackboard was being introduced as their course management system. Conducted by a Blackboard trainer, the session was held in a large auditorium and attended by well over a hundred faculty. In lecture fashion, the trainer introduced the functions of Blackboard through the use of PowerPoint slides. His delivery was dry, and with no way to actually try what he was presenting, faculty in the room were becoming visibly anxious and agitated. Comments such as, "I'll never get this" could be heard in conversations between faculty in conversations both during and after the training. Clearly, this was a case in which teaching methods did not match learning outcomes and served as a poor model of "good" teaching, as well as how that might translate to the online environment.

One of the goals of training for online teaching should be to model the types of teaching techniques that a faculty might use in their own classes. Active, collaborative means of training faculty will help promote the development of a faculty learning community that can continue to serve as a support as faculty begin to teach online. Barlett and Rappaport (2009) state that building community among faculty across departments and schools within the university is one of the most powerful benefits of conducting faculty development programs. The topic of building a faculty learning community is one we explore further in Chapter Five. Training should ideally be set up with a combination of independent activities coupled with group and collaborative activities, providing variety and serving to actively engage participants with one another.

Adults are more receptive to learning in environments that are physically and psychologically comfortable. Many who write about conducting good training emphasize the importance of conducting training in a comfortable environment. Others discuss the importance of providing a meal or snacks. We were working with a faculty developer on a large campus to plan a training program, who mentioned that she always plans training around lunch, as the faculty she works with will always show up for a meal even if they aren't interested in the topic! Although this may be an overstatement, providing food is one way to acknowledge that faculty are taking time from their busy schedules to participate—the food serves as both an incentive and a reward for their expenditure of time.

Zhu (2008) further recommends that training be taken to the faculty rather than having the faculty sit in large computer labs at a central location on campus. Such training can be conducted on a departmental level and can be conducted using master faculty as trainers. Another means by which to take training to the faculty is through the use of online training, a topic to which we will now turn our attention.

ONLINE, FACE-TO-FACE, OR HYBRID: WHICH WORKS BEST?

Hagner (2001) notes that a wide variety exists in how training for online teaching and curriculum development is delivered. He believes that this may be due to the variation in institutional cultures. We contend that this may also be due to the variations in faculty levels of experience with and exposure to the online environment. Regardless, in order to accommodate these variations, there also needs to be a variety of training approaches utilized. People often laugh when we tell them that we are traveling to a given institution to offer training for online instruction, feeling that training for teaching online should be delivered online. To some degree, they are right, but given the level of fear and resistance often experienced by novice and beginning faculty, we find that meeting with them face-to-face to start with reduces their anxiety as well as their resistance. Consequently, we often recommend that an institution start with a face-to-face training and then move training online. Once there is a core group in place that has experienced training, they can be called upon to assist with training other faculty on campus, thus becoming mentors to newer faculty. We have often been asked to develop online training for an institution and find that if we are able to visit first, we are better able to determine the institutional culture, level of online experience that exists there, and what the training needs might be. The exception to this is our extensive online certification program, which draws faculty from many different institutions, where we conduct the program fully online. We discuss the important elements that need to be considered in fully on-line training in Chapter Five, where we review models of hybrid and online training.

Conducting a basic needs assessment before training begins can help those tasked with faculty development—be they staff of the teaching and learning center, faculty members on campus who have been asked to conduct training for online teaching, or individual faculty members attempting to train themselves—to develop a training program that is flexible and adaptive. We present such a needs assessment in Appendix C. In addition to assessing levels of experience, Neal and Peed-Neal (2009) note the importance of becoming familiar with policies that govern the institution's delivery of instruction along with the structure of the organization and administrative concerns. Needs assessments for online training should identify all of the stakeholders—administrators, faculty, staff, and students—and communicate with them along the way in order to develop a good system of training that is responsive to all expressed needs. Given that many of our students are far more experienced with technology than are the faculty working with them in online classes and express disappointment with their online classes as a result, incorporating learner perceptions of what they are looking for and need is crucial (Moore, Moore, & Fowler, 2009).

Our own experience, then, leads us to believe that, if at all possible, the following has the greatest potential for developing excellent online instructors:

- A variety of training options—independent computer-based training, face-to-face seminars, online training experiences that are both synchronous and asynchronous (geographically dispersed faculty can be trained using technology such as web conferencing, web casting, and the like), and more informal discussion opportunities, such as brown bag lunches and online faculty discussions . . .
- Coupled with support and mentoring and . . .
- Developed based on the needs of the institution

This view is supported by Cravener (1998), who talks about the "paradoxical disjunction" between what she terms the information technology approach to faculty development and the psychosocial concerns that can act as barriers to participation by faculty in an online effort. By offering a variety of approaches coupled with support, the barriers to technology integration and online teaching will begin to fall and all of the important elements we have discussed previously—people, pedagogy, content, and technology—have greater likelihood of being addressed.

WHO SHOULD CONDUCT TRAINING FOR ONLINE TEACHING?

Once training needs are assessed and approaches determined, the important question of who should deliver faculty training emerges. Based on a study of faculty developers and their perceptions of their role in the institutions they serve, Mullinix (2008) concluded that holding faculty status on campus increases the credibility of those called upon to conduct faculty development activities. When faculty train faculty, there is likely to be an increased level of trust, credibility, and appreciation for their teaching abilities and instructional design skills. The faculty developers in the study noted that teaching experience should be defined as teaching other faculty, as well as teaching students, and that experience with both enhances credibility. Cravener (1998) notes the importance of identifying trainers who are viewed by the faculty as being role models due to their expertise in both teaching and the use of technology.

We have certainly heard complaints from faculty who were being trained to teach online by a staff person with no teaching experience and have unfortunately experienced some of those training programs ourselves. But we also previously reported on the successful efforts of one university to use graduate students to train faculty in the use of technology in teaching (Palloff & Pratt, 2001). Our own experience has taught us to rely on our graduate students to introduce us to new techniques, such as conducting classes in Second Life or the use of cell phones or Twitter as discussion adjuncts to an online class. When master faculty view themselves as lifelong learners who can learn something new from anyone, including students, the result is the development of new and creative ways to teach online and to maximize learning outcomes.

As with training approaches, flexibility is the key here, along with the reduction of resistance and anxiety. As Hagner (2001) states, "Looking foolish or incompetent in front of their students is an anathema to faculty" (p. 2). If it is likely that a given faculty member will resist working with a student or less experienced staff member for his or her online training, then training should be conducted by another faculty member or someone who holds more credibility. Force-fitting training does not work—adapting training and those who train to training needs is crucial.

In the next chapter, we explore in more depth approaches to training and development for online teaching that incorporate the strategies we have discussed. We believe that these strategies work and work well to develop excellent online instructors and excellent online programs.

KEY POINTS IN TRAINING FOR EXCELLENCE

• Don't use cookie-cutter approaches to faculty training—offer, instead, a flexible schedule and a menu of topics that address the continuum of faculty experience from novice to master.

- Use approaches based on adult learning theory—active approaches that combine individual and collaborative engagement work best.
- Honor experience! Apprentice training is for novices and apprentices, not experienced or master faculty who are changing institutions.
- Use best practices in online teaching in training approaches—model those practices so that faculty can incorporate them into their own courses seamlessly.
- Incorporate cycles of learn, do, reflect into training, allowing faculty to learn about a new skill, practice it, and then reflect on the results.

BECOMING YOUR OWN FACULTY DEVELOPER

After reading about important elements in faculty training, revisit the plan you developed for your own training and ask yourself

- Have I identified colleagues with whom I might establish a relationship for developing our online skills or for support?
- Have I identified a student or two who might be able to help me assess how well I'm using technology in my teaching or who might teach me about particular applications or approaches?
- Have I been able to identify what are considered best practices in online teaching and can I learn more about and model them in my own work?
- How can I establish my own learn, do, reflect cycles in my development?
- How will I know if I'm making progress?

Our advice to you at this juncture is to find trusted colleagues who are also interested in moving their online practice forward. Work to establish a community of practice where you can bounce ideas off of one another and practice your skills. Agree to meet regularly to discuss best practices in online teaching. Finally, don't be afraid to consult with your students or sons and daughters of friends—their opinions and ideas will be invaluable to you as you move forward.

PART TWO   # Supporting the Movement from New to Great

Models of Faculty Development

As we established in the first part of this book, faculty develop-ment is critical to technology integration in face-to-face courses and is particularly so in helping faculty transition to online teaching. We have established a theoretical foundation for training that is based on a developmental framework and adult learning theory. With this foundation in place, we now turn our attention to ways in which training is delivered and address the question: What constitutes an effective training model for faculty development focused on online teaching? In addition to reviewing some existing models for online faculty development in this chapter, the topic of addressing training needs of faculty "across the lifespan" will be discussed. In other words:

- What might a phased approach to faculty development look like?
- What is best incorporated into training for new faculty?
- How can the experience of more seasoned online faculty be honored in training and what are their needs?
- Is a learning community approach appropriate for online faculty development, and how can one be developed and maintained?
- What topics should be addressed in a long-term faculty development effort?

- How can adjuncts at a distance be effectively trained?

- How can training happen efficiently and quickly so as to get faculty into the online classroom with a minimum of delay?

- How effective are certificate programs in online faculty development, and what do certificates mean?

A PHASED APPROACH TO ONLINE FACULTY DEVELOPMENT

As we have already established, effective faculty development for online teaching is not a process that should or does occur in one workshop or one online training course. Given that faculty have training needs that differ according to their phase of development, the focus and content of training needs to align with their position in the developmental lifespan. We are not the only authors to look at a developmental model for faculty development where technology is concerned. Sherry, Billig, Tavalin, and Gibson (2000) studied and presented what they termed the technology learning/adoption trajectory model and proposed training strategies that accompanied each phase in the model. They discuss the following phases and strategies:

- *Stage 1. Teacher as learner:* Termed an information gathering stage, instructors are seeking to develop the skills they need in order to perform instructional tasks using technology. Recommended training includes demonstrations of best practices using technology delivered by peers who are already incorporating technology into teaching.

- *Stage 2. Teacher as adopter:* This is an experimental stage in which instructors try out various forms of technology and share their experiences in doing so with a focus on task management. The use of mentors and knowledgeable peers, as well as lab situations, is recommended to support instructors in their experimentation.

- *Stage 3. Teacher as co-learner:* A clear relationship between technology and the delivery of curriculum is forming at this stage. It is at this point that workshops focusing on enhancing instruction through the use of technology are recommended, along with collegial sharing of lesson and assessment ideas. Students can be effectively used as technical assistants in this phase.

- *Stage 4. Teacher as reaffirmer or rejector:* Greater awareness of learning outcomes is developing in this phase, along with the ability to determine the impact of various technological approaches on student learning. Incentive systems work well at this phase, including encouragement to disseminate exemplary student work as examples of the impact of technology on student progress and performance.

- *Stage 5. Teacher as leader:* Experienced instructors are encouraged to expand their roles in this phase to become active researchers and teach new members. Instead of participating in training at this phase, instructors are encouraged to lead workshops and work as mentors.

Roughly equivalent to the phased model we presented in Chapter Two, this model also provides a framework through which training needs can be addressed. Sherry and colleagues (2000) wait until the third phase to introduce workshops regarding technology integration and online teaching—something we recommend introducing much earlier—and do not specify training strategies for the last two phases. We believe that training should occur throughout the lifespan of the online instructor, however, and should be tailored to the experience level.

Teclehaimanot and Lamb (2005) provide a bridge to the specifics of training by reviewing a three-year professional development program. The program focuses initially on exploration of popular topics and then moves to a hands-on approach and modeling in the first year. In the second year, the emphasis is on individualization of instruction, infusion of technology into the curriculum, and a focus on efficient use of technology. Finally, in the third year, the focus is on the development of a learning community, mentoring, sharing, and increasing levels of motivation to teach with technology. Many institutions do not have the luxury of a three-year period in which to institute an ongoing faculty development effort, or the funding to devote to that effort. What, then, might be created as a series of workshops that address the needs of faculty from visitor to master, as we termed them in Chapter Two, and how can faculty from all phases of development be encouraged to participate? Let's now look at a potential training model (Table 4.1) based on a phased approach that can be dispatched in a shorter period of time to multiple experience categories. Appendix A contains suggested training plans for each format and the topics suggested.

As we have established, the best approach to training includes both face-to-face and online-training options and is based on faculty desires and needs. The approaches presented can be considered a menu of options and topics that can be pulled into a long-term faculty development effort or deployed over a shorter

Table 4.1
Sample Training Model

Target Audience	Format	Time	Topics	Objectives and Outcomes
			Face-to-Face Training	
Visitor/ novice/ beginner	*Face-to-face* workshop followed by individual-ized support and training	3 hours	Introduction to the course management system Best practices in online teaching Use of online discussions Making the transition to online teaching	Reduce fear and resistance and introduce online learning concepts
Beginner/ insider	*Face-to-face* workshop followed by individual-ized support and training	3 to 6 hours	Effective online course design Building online learning communities Assessment Academic integrity online Best practices in online teaching Collaborating online Effective online discussions Hybrid classes	Focus on pedagogy and reinforce best practices in online learning
Insider	*Face-to-face* workshop	3 to 6 hours	Authentic assessment Promoting reflection Virtual teaming Using social networking Technologies Web 2.0 and online teaching	Advance pedagogical skill; link online pedagogy to the discipline; increase technological skill

Table 4.1
(*Continued*)

Target Audience	Format	Time	Topics	Objectives and Outcomes
Insider/ master	*Face-to-face* workshop	3 to 6 hours	Planning effective distance learning programs Faculty leadership Mentoring for online teaching Getting published Effective faculty evaluation	Increase mastery of online teaching skills; promote leadership and mentoring
			Online Training	
All	*Online seminar*	1–2 weeks	Orientation to the institution	Introduce policies and procedures
Novice/ beginner	*Online seminar*	4–6 weeks	See Appendix A for a suggested training plan including these possible beginning topics: Using technology in teaching Effective online facilitation Syllabus development for online teaching Maximizing participation online Online discussion Assessment Beginning course design	Reduce anxiety about technology use; begin to develop best practices in online teaching; begin to establish online presence
Beginner/ insider	*Online Seminar*	2–4 weeks	See Appendix A for a suggested training plan including these possible intermediate topics: Collaboration online Incorporating reflection into online classes	Solidify online presence; link pedagogy and technology to content and the discipline; advance pedagogical skill

(Continued)

Table 4.1
(*Continued*)

Target Audience	Format	Time	Topics	Objectives and Outcomes
			Developing critical thinking skills online Legal and ethical issues (including copyright and fair use) Authentic assessment Content-related seminars	
Insider/ master	*Online Seminar*	Short self-paced modules or 1–2 week online courses	See Appendix A for a suggested training plan including these possible advanced topics: Advanced facilitation skills Advanced technical skills (using audio, video, and Web 2.0 technologies) Content-related seminars	Promote advanced skill development; introduce and practice use of advanced technologies

time to get faculty ready to teach online. For example, an institution planning to jump-start a new online program or significantly expand online offerings they have within a semester or two may decide to offer a one-day face-to-face session followed by four to six weeks online training. This should be coupled with ongoing support for course development and technology integration. A longer-term approach can be added to this once the initial launch has been achieved and should be based on previous planning and vision for the online program as a whole, as well as faculty needs and desires. We now look at what it takes to establish a long-term faculty development effort for online teaching.

ESTABLISHING A LONG-TERM FACULTY DEVELOPMENT EFFORT

Although many academic institutions engage in strategic planning for the institution as a whole and are likely to include discussion of the use of technology, few engage in strategic planning for online learning or technology integration specifically (Levy, 2003). Bates (2000) suggests perhaps "the biggest challenge [in online education] is the lack of vision and the failure to use technology strategically" (p. 7).

Matheson (2006) states the following about strategic planning for online education: "A strategic plan should emphasize not only the immediate institutional needs and priorities—such as developing and updating programs, implementing a curriculum or curricular changes, marketing programs, and preparing for accreditation. It also should acknowledge and help educators plan for changes within the larger 'outside' world of online education" ("Strategic Planning and Trends in Online Education," para. 3). Included in that "outside world" are policy issues, changes in technology, and societal changes and demands.

Matheson further stresses that institutions need to view their online programs as part of an academic whole and not stand-alone efforts. According to Levy (2003), institutions that want to have an effective online program need to consider all aspects of providing an education, which involves more than simply putting classes online. Clearly, an institution needs to understand where online education fits in its vision of the institution's future, its mission, and how it views its faculty and students. Integration of the online program into the institution's larger strategy means that it should be treated as any other curricular effort should be—faculty need to be trained and evaluated as part of a larger institution-wide development effort and also must be involved in the development of every aspect of the program. Furthermore, the strategic plan should go beyond pedagogical changes based on content but should also focus on the impact of new technologies on pedagogy and content. Training efforts with regard to these issues should target all faculty, not just those teaching online.

Questions to consider when planning a long-term faculty development for online teaching include

- What role do online classes play in the larger curriculum?
- What pedagogical methods are being used or recommended?

- What is the experience level of the faculty? What range of training courses (from novice to master) will be necessary?
- Who will conduct training for faculty? What is the budget for training?
- What is the experience level of our students and what are they asking for in terms of online education?
- Who will train and support students?
- Who will support faculty?

Planning a long-term faculty development effort involves looking at more than simply offering training on the use of technology in teaching. It requires forethought and ongoing evaluation to ensure that the needs of all stakeholders are being met. Good planning of the program as a whole, with training as a part of that program, can also help reduce faculty resistance to teaching online by removing the obstacles that often discourage them (Faculty Focus, 2008). Appendix C contains a planning template that provides a place to start when thinking about long-term program planning for online teaching that includes a faculty development component.

THE LEARNING COMMUNITY APPROACH TO ONLINE FACULTY DEVELOPMENT

Another means by which long-term faculty development can be achieved is through the formation and support of communities of practice among faculty. We have long promoted the development and use of a community-based approach to online teaching (Palloff & Pratt, 1999, 2007). One of the most effective ways to assist faculty in understanding the value of a learning community in online teaching is to incorporate this same approach into faculty training and development.

Twale and De Luca (2008) discuss the competitive nature of academic life. They state, "While institutions and university faculty may value, reward, and welcome collaboration with colleagues and students, a professional reputation is gained in singular fashion through a research agenda, perhaps of first or singularly authored publications in prestigious journals" (p. 67). Couple this with the precarious position online teaching holds with regard to tenure and promotion in many institutions and the result is a situation that could potentially discourage engagement not only in online teaching but also in collaboration with colleagues for training purposes. Our experience has shown us, however, that less competition seems to exist in the online world. Perhaps because online teaching creates a disorienting dilemma for many, faculty are more willing to share their successes with their colleagues along with suggestions for overcoming challenges. Repositories for learning objects, such as Merlot or WebQuest.org, exist for the sole purpose of sharing teaching strategies that work. Capitalizing on this can be a catalyst to the development of a community of practice to support online teaching in an institution. How, then, can a learning community be formed that supports the training and development of those faculty who are teaching either hybrid or online?

Faculty learning communities can be established on the basis of the academic year, asking faculty to join at the start, should they be interested, for a semester or the full academic year. Cohorts can be formed to accommodate groups of faculty. Or groups can be formed around a topic of interest (Nugent, Reardon, Smith, Rhodes, Zander, & Carter, 2008). Using the same technologies employed for delivering online or hybrid classes at an institution can be a start. Discussion forums for faculty, listservs, chat, webcasts, synchronous sessions in a virtual classroom setting, and the development of blogs and wikis can create ways in which faculty can communicate and collaborate. Just as a blended approach to training for online teaching appears to be the most effective, a blended approach to creating a faculty community of practice seems potentially equally effective (Vaughan, 2004). Initial face-to-face sessions can be the impetus to begin a formal faculty learning community or can trigger the development of ad hoc learning communities. The community can be sustained by online communication, project-based work, and discussion of readings, and other activities can help keep the discussion going over time.

Our own framework of an online learning community (Palloff & Pratt, 2007) can be applied to online faculty development. The essential components of that framework include people, purpose, and process, leading to an outcome of reflection and transformation. When applied to a faculty learning community formed for the purpose of faculty development, the framework would look as it does in Figure 4.1.

What is important to remember is that due to faculty workloads and time constraints, engaging in online communication with other faculty members

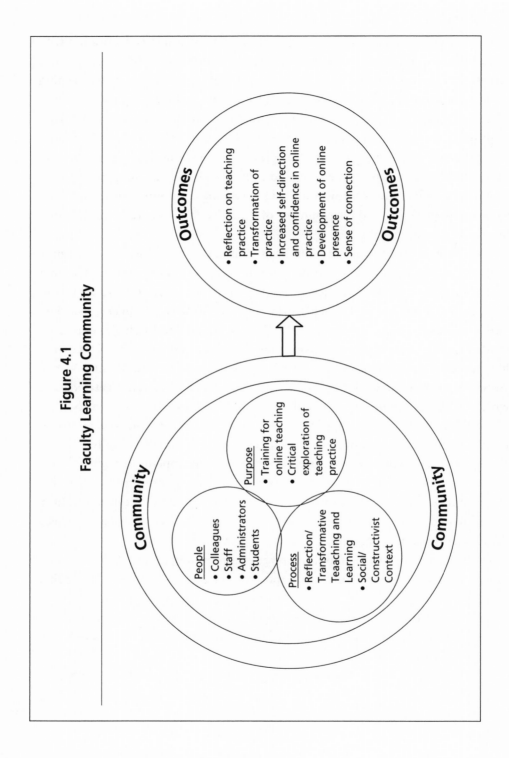

Figure 4.1
Faculty Learning Community

Outcomes

- Reflection on teaching practice
- Transformation of practice
- Increased self-direction and confidence in online practice
- Development of online presence
- Sense of connection

Outcomes

Community

Community

People
- Colleagues
- Staff
- Administrators
- Students

Purpose
- Training for online teaching
- Critical exploration of teaching practice

Process
- Reflection/ Transformative Teaaching and Learning
- Social/ Constructivist Context

(clearly the *people* component) needs to have a *purpose*. The purpose cannot simply be training and development, but should also focus on critical exploration of teaching practice for hybrid and online teaching. Consequently, bringing the members of the community together at the start to negotiate its purpose and how members will engage with one another (or the *process*) is extremely important. In addition, members need to engage in dialogue about the topics they wish to explore, the time they are willing to put into the activity, how long the community will stay together, and so forth. Just as in an online course, producing a group charter or a set of guidelines is key to the success of the faculty learning community.

An example of a successful faculty learning community is Jamestown Community College in New York. To begin with, 14 members of the Jamestown faculty entered and completed the Teaching in the Virtual Classroom certificate program at Fielding Graduate University. During the time that they were in the program, they began meeting for brown-bag lunch sessions to discuss what they were learning and how they were applying that knowledge in their own teaching. Once the program ended, the brown-bag sessions, along with online communication continued—the participants found that they enjoyed the ongoing support the sessions provided and the creative thinking that was triggered as a result. Not only does the learning community approach provide ongoing training and support for faculty with minimal budget expenditure, it also provides the experience of a way in which education can happen with students, thus allowing transfer of the approach learned into classes taught.

WORKING WITH ADJUNCTS AT A DISTANCE

Because adjunct faculty are often discipline-specific professionals first and instructors second, Lorenzetti (2009) speculates that a potential weakness for them is a lack of training in pedagogical theory. This can result in a negative impact not only on student retention and success, but the attrition of adjuncts as well. Although this may not be true for all adjuncts, they need to be brought into any faculty development efforts for online teaching that are offered either on campus or online, and orientation for adjuncts should be mandatory before they start teaching in an online program. In so doing, adjuncts can and should become part of the community-based approach to training while developing a connection to the institution and increasing their level of teaching skill. Velez (2009) notes that many faculty can and do create full-time careers by teaching online for multiple institutions. She further notes that once these adjuncts have received technical training and support, their need for such services declines. However, their need for collegiality and connection continues. Velez states, "since no study [has] confirmed how online faculty operationalize the construct of collegiality, universities may not be doing it right or doing it at all" (p. 1). Our own experiences as online adjuncts confirms this observation—rarely are adjuncts offered ongoing training for online teaching and rarely are they brought into decisions regarding program structure and design, governance, and the like. The result is a rather disconnected and isolated faculty body with little insight into how to get help when needed, how to deal with difficult students, or how to seek additional training should that be desired.

Involving online adjuncts in faculty communities of practice is one way to provide the ongoing training and connection they need. In addition, such an approach is likely to improve faculty performance through ongoing discussion of teaching practice and allowing a venue to bring up difficult issues as they arise. It also allows the university to more easily convey new expectations for practice, introduce new technologies, and better ensure that those practices are being integrated into teaching through ongoing discussion. Including adjuncts in the faculty learning community further ensures loyalty to the institution by helping them feel like they belong to a place, even if that place is virtual—an important aspect of community-building. Many times, institutions assume that their adjunct faculty do not want to be involved in ongoing training and discussion; however, our discussions with adjuncts have proven just the opposite. All administrators need to do is ask—they're likely to be surprised by the results! Providing other forms of incentive for adjuncts can also help bring them into the faculty learning community. Adjuncts appreciate stipends for course development, assistance with payment of fees for conference attendance, and even small tokens of appreciation such as certificates and items that contain university logos, such as T-shirts and coffee mugs. All of this simply lets adjunct instructors know that the work they are doing is important to the institution and that their contributions are valued.

TRAINING EFFICIENTLY

One concern that is often expressed to us is that it can take upward of a semester to adequately prepare a faculty member to teach online. We have been asked, "Isn't there a way to speed up this process and move faculty into online courses as the need presents?" The answer to this question is not a simple one and is dependent on a number of factors, such as faculty level of experience with technology and online teaching and whether or not courses are prewritten or need to be developed.

If an institution is in the process of developing its online program and does not have preexisting courses that an adjunct or core faculty member can simply start teaching, then time needs to be allocated for course development. The generally agreed-upon time frame for course development is approximately one semester prior to the start of that course. Those with experience in course development may be able to create a course in a shorter period of time. However, novices and beginners often need at least that much time, and sometimes more, to put a course together, learn the course management system through which the course is to be delivered, and develop effective facilitation skills as well. Those faculty who are more experienced with online teaching may not need to focus on facilitation skills but may still need the course development time.

Many institutions are moving to prewritten courses that can be delivered by a number of faculty members in a given discipline or content area in order to have an online program that is scalable. In this case, training effort is focused on the technology in use and facilitation skills used to disseminate the class. When faculty have some experience with online teaching and a class is prewritten, they can be ready to teach in a very short period—some institutions deliver such training in an online training class that might last from one to four weeks. Figure 4.2 illustrates the differences in the two types of programs we've been discussing and the rapidity with which faculty can be prepared to begin teaching.

Unforeseen circumstances do occur—a need for an extra section of a class or a faculty member unable to teach at the last minute, for example—but a well-planned online program with a variety of training options and a well-trained cadre of faculty should be able to address those problems quickly. Just as faculty must be flexible in the delivery of their courses, the program itself should be flexible enough to move an experienced faculty member directly to online courses with a minimum of training time.

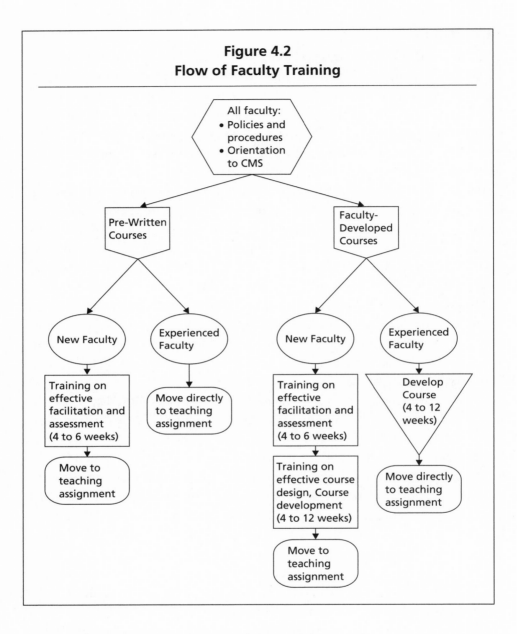

Figure 4.2
Flow of Faculty Training

All faculty:
• Policies and procedures
• Orientation to CMS

Pre-Written Courses

Faculty-Developed Courses

New Faculty

Experienced Faculty

New Faculty

Experienced Faculty

Training on effective facilitation and assessment (4 to 6 weeks)

Move directly to teaching assignment

Training on effective facilitation and assessment (4 to 6 weeks)

Develop Course (4 to 12 weeks)

Move to teaching assignment

Training on effective course design, Course development (4 to 12 weeks)

Move directly to teaching assignment

Move to teaching assignment

CERTIFICATE PROGRAMS IN ONLINE TEACHING

As hybrid and online programs have grown, the demand to "certify" faculty to teach online has emerged. At the time of this writing, there are no standards for online instructors in higher education, although there are standards that are proposed for K–12 education. The North American Council for Online Learning (2009) has published a set of potential standards for online teaching and instructional design. Designed for states, school districts, online programs, and other organizations, the standards measure quality and provide a rating scale ranging from absent (a particular component is missing) to very satisfactory (meaning that no improvement is needed). Unlike the Quality Matters rubric, which focuses on instructional design, the standards focus on the instructor, his or her qualifications to teach online, and the manner in which he or she delivers instruction. The standards include the following major categories and several substandards contained within them:

- The teacher meets the professional teaching standards established by a state licensing agency or the teacher has academic credentials in the field in which he or she is teaching.
- The teacher has the prerequisite technology skills to teach online.
- The teacher plans, designs, and incorporates strategies to encourage active learning, interaction, participation, and collaboration in the online environment.
- The teacher provides online leadership in a manner that promotes student success through regular feedback, prompt response, and clear expectations.
- The teacher models, guides, and encourages legal, ethical, safe, and healthy behavior related to technology use.
- The teacher has experienced online learning from the perspective of a student.
- The teacher understands and is responsive to students with special needs in the online classroom.
- The teacher demonstrates competencies in creating and implementing assessments in online learning environments in ways that ensure validity and reliability of instruments and procedures.
- The teacher develops and delivers assessments, projects, and assignments that meet standards-based learning goals and assesses learning progress by measuring student achievement of learning goals.
- The teacher demonstrates competencies in using data and findings from assessments and other data sources to modify instructional methods and content and to guide student learning.

- The teacher demonstrates frequent and effective strategies that enable both teacher and students to complete self- and pre-assessments (i.e., assesses readiness for course content and method of delivery).
- The teacher collaborates with colleagues.
- The teacher arranges media and content to help students and teachers transfer knowledge most effectively in the online environment.

The standards in their entirety effectively define the characteristics and behaviors of the excellent online instructor. Many certification programs are based on several of these standards, but without a uniform and accepted approach to certification at present, the programs that exist vary widely in terms of content and quality. Despite this, participation in a certification program does ensure that the instructor has, at the very least, been involved in an online program as a student that explores best practices in online teaching, giving him or her a leg up with a potential employer or on his or her own campus.

KEY POINTS REGARDING MODELS OF ONLINE FACULTY DEVELOPMENT

- Training for online teaching should be developed to correspond to the phases in which faculty find themselves—in other words, training experiences should be developed that span the continuum from little to no online experience to those who are master instructors online.
- Topics for training should respond to faculty interest and needs. Surveying faculty to determine how much experience they have and what their training needs might be is a good way to start.
- Use a learning community approach to training to model the development of a learning community in an online course and to sustain faculty development efforts.
- Include adjuncts in training and in the faculty learning community to increase levels of adjunct faculty loyalty and connection, as well as increasing their performance.
- Plan, plan, plan faculty development efforts well in advance!
- Train efficiently by charting the flow of training from orientation to the point of course delivery and be flexible in moving faculty through the process.

- Encourage faculty to enroll in certification programs or create a certification program on campus to ensure that faculty receive training in best practices for online teaching.

BECOMING YOUR OWN FACULTY DEVELOPER

If a learning community effort does not exist on your campus, consider being the one to start one. You can connect with your colleagues to start brown-bag lunch discussions on topics of interest to those teaching online, set up online discussion groups and forums, and initiate collaborative training projects. The only issue to consider is time, since free online resources for discussion are widely available. Reach out to your colleagues and see who responds—you may find that there are several people on your campus or in your institution who are interested in coming together to explore online teaching practice.

Consider, also, enrolling in a certification program for online teaching. In so doing, you will be able to experience an online course from the perspective of a student and, in some cases, also from the perspective of the instructor. You will also be interacting with like-minded colleagues from many institutions, which will expand your network of peers and help you create a more extensive community of practice. Also consider attending online conferences on topics related to online teaching. Most certification programs and online conferences are affordable—even if you're unable to get faculty development funding from your institution, you should be able to access these programs without much financial strain and may also be able to earn continuing education units or graduate-level credit that may help you advance. A listing of some certification programs can be found in Appendix B.

Mentoring Online Faculty

Mentoring is commonly viewed as a promising strategy through which new faculty are oriented to their institutions and to teaching (Yun & Scorcinelli, 2009). Weimer (2009) notes that not only do those who are mentored benefit from a mentoring relationship, but the mentor also benefits from the interaction. Effective mentoring for new instructors in the face-to-face environment is seen as having the impact of reducing professional isolation, providing support and feedback on performance, and helping mentees achieve greater levels of confidence in their teaching (Mohono-Mahlatsi & van Tonder, 2006). When it comes to teaching with technology, however, the understanding of the role of mentoring is not quite so clear (Boulay & Fulford, 2009). Because faculty who are new to teaching online need examples, models, and individualized support, a number of institutions are now turning to mentoring programs to meet that need.

Institutions, such as Florida State College at Jacksonville and Park University in Missouri, have adopted mentoring programs as a means of orienting online faculty, providing ongoing training and development, and retaining faculty. Creating a mentoring relationship through the pairing of faculty who are more experienced online with those who are just starting helps break down barriers and provides real, concrete examples of what works and what does not. Studies on faculty development through mentoring reveal that without the support of a more experienced colleague to guide them, many faculty would most likely have discontinued their involvement with online teaching beyond their first course (Mandernach, Donelli, Dailey & Schulte, 2005). Using a mentoring approach to the training of online instructors can help determine who will succeed and who might not be well suited to teaching online, given that mentors may also be asked to play the role of assessors of their mentees. We review mentoring approaches in this chapter along with suggestions for the development of effective mentoring programs.

COMMON ELEMENTS OF MENTORING APPROACHES

Chuang, Thompson, and Schmidt (2003) reviewed the literature on technology mentoring programs for faculty and found that all programs and approaches discussed included several common elements: providing visions for technology use; individualizing technology support; breaking down hierarchical structure; establishing open dialogue and collaborative relationships; providing mutual benefits for mentors and mentees; and emphasizing the creation of a learning community for those participating in the program. Let's look at each element and how a mentoring program might address them.

Providing Visions for Technology Use

Novice instructors often have difficulty seeing the myriad ways that technology might be infused into their teaching. As we have discussed, this along with fear of the technology itself are some of the needs that novice faculty have as they begin to move into online teaching. By working collaboratively with a mentor or a peer group, novice faculty can begin to "catch the vision" in terms of ways in which technology might enhance the work they do with students, as well as develop understanding of the pedagogy involved in online teaching. Chuang, Thompson, and Schmidt (2003) noted that faculty who completed mentoring programs indicated that they were able to gain a deeper level of understanding in terms of how to use technology effectively along with a greater sense of confidence in their ability to do so.

Individualizing Technology Support

Individualized support, such as that offered through a mentoring relationship, provides learner-focused instruction. Given that a learner-focused approach is what we promote for online teaching, doesn't it make sense to provide the same to those who are learning how to do it? Working with a mentor to learn how to use technology and teach online allows the new online instructor to work at his or her own pace while allowing for the specific needs of an instructor's discipline or teaching approach. Furthermore, providing an individualized approach reduces perceived risk on the part of the new instructor, by allowing experimentation and exploration without feeling or looking foolish in front of a group of students. This approach allows the instructor to practice and make mistakes before "going live" with a group of students in an online class. Often this involves first shadowing a more experienced instructor in his or her online course, followed by the mentor shadowing the new instructor as he or she teaches for the first time. Observations should be coupled with ongoing discussion about technique and designed to support any needed changes. What should be avoided, however, is putting the mentor in an evaluative position in terms of job performance or job retention. Feedback should be for the purpose of performance and quality improvement.

Breaking Down Hierarchical Structure

Group and network approaches and the use of students as mentors help break down the traditional hierarchical structures that exist with traditional mentoring. When a more experienced instructor is assigned to a novice instructor for mentoring purposes, a power imbalance is established. There is also an inherent risk when mentors are assigned rather than chosen that the individuals involved will not develop a strong relationship resulting in the desired outcomes (Goodyear, 2006). When group and network approaches are used, however, mentees often set the direction of mentoring, determine the norms by which the group will operate, and set the agenda for the group. Not dependent on a one-to-one relationship, mentees are able to get needs met from multiple sources and power imbalances are erased, thus resulting in a more collaborative, community-oriented approach. This is particularly important when students are used as mentors—they need to feel comfortable approaching their mentees on equal footing in order to support them in learning about and using technology effectively.

Establishing Open Dialogue and Collaborative Relationships

When nonhierarchical models are employed for mentoring, the result is often increased levels of mutual respect and trust (Chuang, Thompson, & Schmidt, 2003). It is not uncommon to see mentees engaging in collaborative work with one another as they become more comfortable in their use of technology—we have seen the development of wikis, projects in Second Life, coteaching, coauthoring articles, and copresenting at conferences resulting from group and network mentoring programs and have often seen such collaborations between faculty members and their student mentors. In fact, we have also benefited from such collaborations when we have worked with our own students to learn a new form of technology. Most recently, we collaborated with a graduate student to support our faculty training and development work with a group of K–12 math teachers. Our student has developed significant expertise in the use of cell phones in his math classes—something he is now teaching us. We brought him into an online training to present his work in this area and also to support the teachers in their exploration of constructivist approaches to math instruction. His involvement was extremely positive and moved the group much farther in their acceptance and understanding of this approach than if we had worked with them by ourselves.

Providing Mutual Benefits for Mentors and Mentees

All of the literature we have reviewed on mentoring, along with our own experiences in this area, underscores that mentoring processes benefit everyone who participates in them—whether mentor or mentee. Whether helping or being helped, self-esteem and confidence increase along with mutual respect. All parties feel a sense of empowerment as well and feel as if they are able to influence those who will carry on in the profession (Goodyear, 2006). Bright (2008) suggests that the collaboration can also create a greater sense of ownership of the institution's online program and greater willingness to participate in evaluation activities, a topic we discuss further in the next chapter. Consequently, not only do mentoring programs benefit those who participate, they also have the potential to benefit the institution as a whole and support their efforts to implement and grow online learning programs.

Emphasizing the Creation of a Learning Community

The positive benefits and outcomes of mentoring that we have been describing—increased collaboration, willingness to experiment with new approaches, mutual respect and trust, mutual learning goals, reduction of hierarchy, and open communication—are all important elements involved in the development of a learning community. Add to that the fact that online teaching can be a very lonely endeavor. Creating a learning community through mentoring relationships can significantly reduce isolation and create a stronger sense of connection to the institution—something that is particularly important for adjuncts at a distance.

Establishing and promoting a mentoring program for online teaching can help infuse a learning community approach into training and, thus, into teaching in the online environment. If we teach the way we were taught, and if we are taught differently as we move into online teaching, the end result is likely to be a more learner-focused, constructivist approach and the development of truly excellent online instructors. We now turn to proposed ways in which mentoring programs can be developed and implemented in the institution to support these goals.

APPROACHES TO MENTORING FOR ONLINE TEACHING

Mentoring programs for technology use and online teaching take several forms. The most common is matching a more experienced insider or master faculty with a novice or beginner, mirroring mentoring programs commonly seen in face-to-face teaching. This approach to mentoring is typically seen as hierarchical—an older, more experienced faculty member is paired with a younger, entry-level faculty member (Zachary, 2000). Given, however, that master online faculty may be more experienced than their novice peers, but not necessarily older, hierarchical models for mentoring online instructors may not be applicable.

Other models of mentoring include informal or ad hoc arrangements in which insider or master faculty volunteer to mentor novice faculty as they express interest in attempting online teaching or in which novice faculty may approach a more experienced peer to request help. Often these relationships may emerge as the result of participation in a face-to-face training on campus or online communication on a faculty forum or listserv. They may not be formalized in an administrative sense but do still serve the purpose of providing modeling and support for novice faculty.

Yet another means by which mentoring occurs, and a significant departure from hierarchical mentoring models, is through the use of students as mentors. Some institutions are pairing undergraduate or graduate students with faculty members. The student's role in the relationship is to assist the faculty member in using and integrating technology. Often the student benefits from learning more about teaching in the process. The student-as-mentor approach has also been used with secondary school students acting as mentors. The Generation YES (Youth & Educators Succeeding) program, which began in 1996 in Olympia, Washington, trains students from grades 8 through 12 to act as mentors for K–12 teachers to assist with technology integration and to help them meet state level technology standards. Considered an exemplary program by the United States Department of Education, evaluation research concluded that the program had significant impact on technology integration on the part of participating teachers while documenting substantial learning gains on the part of the school-age mentors (Generation www.Y, n.d., Evidence of Effectiveness, para. 1–4).

Mentoring does not necessarily need to occur in a one-to-one relationship. Earlier in this book, we made reference to group approaches to mentoring. Gray and Birch (2008) discuss one such approach wherein a group of new faculty would mentor one another while seeking out individual mentoring relationships with more seasoned faculty. Although an interesting approach, this may not be as effective with online faculty who may be struggling to learn the use of technology and may not be able, therefore, to guide one another. However, group approaches to mentoring for online teaching do have merit.

Goodyear (2006) describes the developmental network, which shifts the focus of mentoring directly to the mentee. In this form of mentoring, mentees would develop their own networks in response to their particular needs; these networks are likely to change over time as the mentee's needs and experience level change. Mentees, in this case, might reach out to a number of people to help them with various functions and skills, as shown in Figure 5.1.

The networked form of group mentoring is particularly beneficial to those who do not have formal mentoring or faculty development programs at their institutions. By first assessing their individual needs, faculty at any level of development can identify and reach out to those who would best meet those needs. Mentoring might take the form of a one-time conversation on a particular issue, an ongoing e-mail or phone discussion, or regular face-to-face meetings when needs arise. Goodyear notes that the ability to reach out to a diverse group of individuals from various institutions, backgrounds, professions, and the like helps create a much broader perspective than if the mentoring relationship exists only between two people. Coupling this approach with group peer mentoring has the potential to create an extremely strong mentoring program—an approach we discuss in more detail later in this chapter.

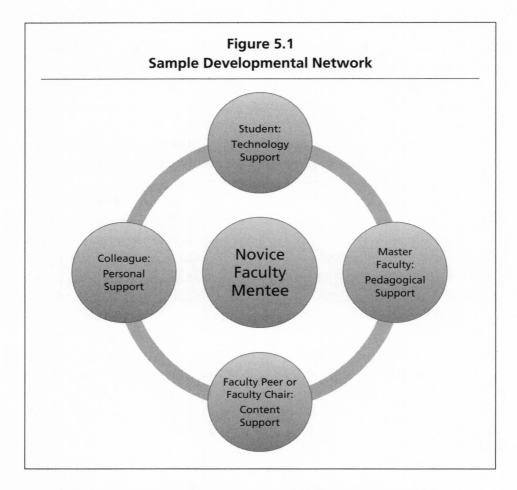

Figure 5.1
Sample Developmental Network

Student: Technology Support

Colleague: Personal Support

Novice Faculty Mentee

Master Faculty: Pedagogical Support

Faculty Peer or Faculty Chair: Content Support

DEVELOPING AN EFFECTIVE MENTORING PROGRAM

Given the potential benefits that mentoring provides for new online instructors, developing a mentoring program as part of faculty development simply makes sense. Combining all or some of the approaches to mentoring also makes sense in terms of providing the greatest level of support, technical skill development, and connection to the institution. Consequently, we propose the following as a possible format for a mentoring program, which can be modified, expanded, or contracted based on institutional culture and budgetary constraints. The program we propose consists of a combination of individual, group, and network approaches.

Plan the Program

The first step in implementing a mentoring program on campus or at a distance is to incorporate the program into the strategic plan for the institution or the strategic plan for technology integration. The questions that need to be addressed and answered include

- What purpose will the mentoring program serve? What is the intent?
- Do we have insider and master faculty available to serve as mentors?
- What modes of communication do we have available to support the mentoring program (i.e., phone, e-mail, instant messaging, web-conferencing, and the like)? What communication tools are commonly used in our environment?
- How many faculty will need mentoring?
- What should the program look like at our institution? Should we match mentors to mentees for one-to-one mentoring? Should we set up groups with one mentor? Should we allow mentees to determine their own forms of mentoring and support the development of networks? Do we want a combination of all of these approaches?
- Will we be able to provide stipends or other incentives to mentors? What level of commitment to the program will we require?

Addressing these questions and more will provide the foundation of and direction for the program. Surveying faculty about their needs is a good place to begin, and factoring their needs into program design is likely to meet with success.

Begin with Mentor Training

Regardless of the form the program takes, those who will serve as mentors on a formal or informal basis need training and preparation before they are called upon to mentor. Topics to consider in training include

- Adult learning theory and adult development
- Faculty leadership
- Knowing thyself: What strengths do I bring to the mentoring relationship and what are some areas of need? Where can I be most helpful?

- Requirements of mentors and the nature of the mentoring program
- Establishing and maintaining a mentoring relationship
- Effective communication skills
- Professional socialization—acclimating the mentee to the institution and the profession
- Mentoring the struggling mentee
- Planning and monitoring progress
- Modeling technology use
- Effective online teaching skills

Mentor training can be delivered in either hybrid or online fashion over a period of four to six weeks. Once a mentor is trained, he or she can then facilitate training courses for a group of mentees, be assigned to a single mentee, or be available to be part of a network of potential mentors.

"Market" and Evaluate the Program

Novice and beginner faculty who are entering online teaching need to know what training they will be expected to complete, as well as the nature of the mentoring program they are entering. Just as the benefits and requirements of mentoring are communicated to the mentors, the requirements of mentees also need to be communicated, as well as the positive benefits participation is likely to yield. In many mentoring programs, mentors and mentees sign mentoring contracts; although this is more important in one-to-one mentoring relationships, an agreement to participate in training and mentoring is a good idea as it clearly delineates responsibilities.

Participating faculty, both mentors and mentees, should track their activities along the way and should also be asked at intervals to evaluate the effectiveness of their participation on their teaching and use of technology. Mentees who are creating a developmental network can use a coaching and mentoring plan (please see an example in Appendix A) to keep track of their felt needs for mentoring, the person they have designated to help address that need, and the activities being used to address it. This should be a fluid plan that changes as progress is made and new needs are identified. It can also provide a good source of evaluation data as time progresses.

Program Format

As mentioned, the most effective mentoring program will contain elements of one-to-one mentoring, with mentors either chosen or assigned; group mentoring; and mentoring through a developmental network. Figure 5.2 illustrates how the program is designed.

Combining all approaches is likely to meet a variety of needs while assisting novice and beginning online faculty to make the transition to online teaching successfully. In addition, combining approaches provides new faculty with exposure to multiple people with a variety of skills and expertise in different areas, thus allowing them to develop a variety of skills and abilities in a shorter period of time.

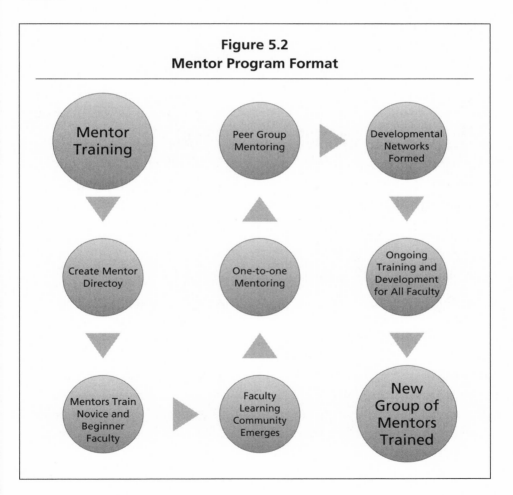

Figure 5.2
Mentor Program Format

Mentor Training

Peer Group Mentoring

Developmental Networks Formed

Create Mentor Directoy

One-to-one Mentoring

Ongoing Training and Development for All Faculty

Mentors Train Novice and Beginner Faculty

Faculty Learning Community Emerges

New Group of Mentors Trained

WHAT ORGANIZATIONS CAN DO TO PROMOTE MENTORING

Zachary (2000) talks about the importance of creating a sustainable mentoring program. She contends that in order to do so, the organization or institution needs to embed mentoring an organizational culture that values continuous learning. She presents ten signs that indicate that a mentoring culture is present:

- *Accountability*—with an eye toward continuous quality improvement, the mentoring program is evaluated regularly, progress is benchmarked, and results are communicated.

- *Alignment*—mentoring is embedded in the culture and not seen as an additional activity; high priority is placed on learning.

- *Demand*—people want to participate in the program either as mentors or mentees and seek out both informal and formal opportunities to do so.

- *Infrastructure*—human and financial resources support the program.

- *A common mentoring vocabulary*—people throughout the organization speak positively about the program, value mentoring experiences, and seek out additional resources and opportunities for learning.

- *Multiple venues*—a combination of mentoring options are available.

- *Reward*—bonuses and stipends are offered to mentors; recognition for participation occurs.

- *Role modeling*—excellence in mentoring is visible in the organization and successes are publicly shared.

- *Safety net*—support is readily available.

- *Training and education*—training and education are strategically linked as part of an overall plan; skill building and renewal training for both mentors and mentees is part of the program (pp. 177–178).

Overall, organizations can promote mentoring by supporting mentoring efforts and building them into their faculty development plans. Even when budgets are tight, mentoring can happen to support the development of high-quality online teaching by making use of the resources provided by master faculty. Recognizing their contributions as mentors is invaluable.

KEY POINTS ABOUT MENTORING ONLINE FACULTY

- Mentoring programs have been shown to be effective in promoting technology integration and online teaching.

- Mentoring programs can take several forms—individual one-to-one mentoring with mentors assigned to or chosen by the mentee, peer mentoring, group mentoring, and networked mentoring. All are effective—choosing a mentoring approach should depend on budget resources and organizational culture.

- Regardless of the method of mentoring chosen, training for mentors should be available to help them be as effective as they can be.

- Top-down approaches to mentoring and assigned mentors seem to be the least effective of the mentoring approaches. More recent mentoring practice favors mentoring that is nonhierarchical, infused into the organizational culture, and flexible over time.

- Both mentors and mentees benefit from mentoring relationships. When students are used as mentors, they gain exposure to teaching practice and also demonstrate their own learning gains.

- Mentoring programs support the development of faculty learning communities, as well as supporting collaborative work among faculty members.

- Mentoring programs, along with the development and maintenance of faculty learning communities, can help reduce faculty isolation and provide a point of connection to the institution for adjunct faculty.

- As with any faculty development effort, a mentoring program should be well planned and evaluated regularly.

BECOMING YOUR OWN FACULTY DEVELOPER

At the end of Chapter Two we asked you to determine your training needs and begin the development of an action plan to meet those needs. We'd like you to revisit that plan and, based on the needs you determined that you had, begin to think about who in your larger network you might be able to contact to mentor you around each need. In Appendix A, you'll find an Individual Faculty Training Plan that asks you to identify a member of your network, the mentoring function that person will serve for you, and the potential activities you might ask that person to engage in with you. In addition, at the end of Chapter Four, we asked you to identify people you could include in a learning community. Think of this group as a peer mentoring group: What topics or activities might you engage in together that would further your mutual needs and skills? How might you include members of your network to support all of the members of your mentoring group? Add those ideas to the second part of the Individual Training Plan. Then set timelines for yourself in terms of when you will contact the people you've identified and when you will get started on your mentoring plan. Remember that your needs will change over time—the sooner you get started on this initial plan, the better!

The Widening Gap
Professional Development
for K–12 Teachers

A large gap has opened that is creating a significant professional development challenges, opportunities, and problems for K–12 teachers and those in higher education who prepare them to teach. The National Education Association (NEA) (n.d.) in its *Guide to Teaching Online Courses* states, "We are preparing teachers for a new generation of learners who grew up with computer and internet technology—millennial learners who use technology in all aspects of their lives, but who still see little significant use of technology to extend their classroom learning" (p. 3). Not unlike students in higher education, K–12 students and their teachers have a perception gap in terms of what teachers think they are providing and students think they are receiving in terms of technology integration in teaching and the quality of online classes. Furthermore, higher education students who are in teacher preparation programs, many of whom are themselves millennial learners, rarely see effective technology integration in the programs that are designed to teach them how to teach. Programs often do not include courses about online teaching and learning or courses conducted online. The result—teachers who are ill prepared to teach the students they face on a daily basis.

The delivery of online classes in the K–12 sector is increasing dramatically, promoting a need for the inclusion of training for online teaching in teacher training programs. James Lehman, project director of the PT3 Program at Purdue University is quoted as saying, "if our student teachers only see faculty members lecturing, they're likely to just lecture. But if they see their faculty members using technology in effective ways, they're going to use technology in effective ways as well" ("Preparing Tomorrow's Teachers to Use Technology," 2002, p. 1). Couple this with demands of teachers by the states in which they teach to be technologically competent, and a significant professional development issue emerges.

As with instructors in higher education, encouraging teachers and teacher educators to incorporate technology into their teaching or to teach online can be met with resistance and challenge. Teachers work in a predominantly teacher-centered environment with highly structured days and little free time, and they spend time at home working on lesson preparation and assessment of student work, leaving little time to pursue their own training for online teaching. Add to that a sense of comfort with the way things have always gone in their classrooms, courses that are developed based on the textbook being used, and state competencies that must be met and measured through standardized testing and room for professional development for online teaching seems to completely vanish ("Preparing Tomorrow's Teachers to Use Technology," 2002). Regardless, the demand for technology integration into K–12 teaching along with the demand for online classes is not diminishing.

Deubel (2008) reports that the demand for "virtual schooling" is increasing at a rate of about 30% per year and with that comes the demand for experienced teachers who can teach online. Watson and Kalmon (2006) further report that as of 2006, there were 24 state-led virtual schools and 12 additional states in the process of developing them. Like their counterparts in higher education, teachers need training in the theoretical, pedagogical, and technical foundations of online work. They also need to understand how to effectively facilitate an online class, including developing effective discussions, managing learners, incorporating collaborative activities, and conducting online assessments of student work. However, DiPietro, Ferdig, Black, and Preston (2008) note that published guidelines aimed at providing K–12 teachers with information on best practices in online teaching often refer to an adaptation of face-to-face teaching techniques and practices or are based on what is required for postsecondary teaching. They contend that little is available to assist K–12 online teachers in understanding effective instructional practices for online teaching in that realm. To better understand the challenges for K–12 teachers, first we look at how online classes are delivered in that sector and then we explore the characteristics of excellent instruction in K–12 classes, and the means by which professional development occurs. Finally, we will circle back to the issues and challenges facing K–12 teachers with suggestions for effectively dealing with those challenges in order to provide excellent online instruction to students.

ONLINE TEACHING METHODS IN THE K–12 ENVIRONMENT

As in higher education, online teaching in K–12 occurs through synchronous and asynchronous means. According to a report issued by the International Association of K–12 Online Learning (iNACOL) (2009), online programs use a variety of means by which education is delivered; however, there has been little research to determine which methods are most successful at this level.

For the most part, virtual schools rely on asynchronous technologies in order to accommodate school schedules and to individualize pacing of the delivery of content. In some cases, a combination of these technologies is used, with some tutoring and discussion held in synchronous virtual classrooms. Scheduling and pacing generally coincide with the school year, with some virtual schools operating on an open or year-round schedule.

Similar to higher education, student-teacher communication generally takes the form of e-mail exchanges and course discussion boards. Some virtual schools require regular phone communication between teacher and students or participation in synchronous sessions via virtual classroom or chat to accomplish the same. Also similar to higher education are many of the roles and tasks of the instructor, including facilitation of instruction by asynchronous or synchronous means, leading discussions, and assessing student performance. One difference is that online K–12 teachers are also expected to conduct regular tutoring sessions with students, which are generally held at scheduled times and generally run through synchronous media.

Virtual school programs can be fully online or hybrid or blended approaches. There are three main models used: blended, supplemental, and classroom-based (Van Dusen, 2009):

- *Blended models.* Often used by charter schools or in homeschooling approaches, the blended model allows students to work from home in online classes for the majority of their work, but students do come into a face-to-face classroom setting with the same instructor for a short period each week.

- *Supplemental models.* This approach allows school districts or multiple districts to fill in curricular gaps through the use of online courses. In this case, students are predominantly in the face-to-face classroom but may take an online course or two in order to move beyond what might be offered at their school. In general, this approach has been used to fill the gaps caused by budget cuts, which have predominantly affected the ability to offer electives, advanced placement courses, language courses, and the like. In addition, supplemental models have been used for the provision of summer school programs and for credit retrieval for students who are in need of credit toward graduation.

- *Classroom-based models.* This approach focuses on technology integration in the face-to-face classroom. However, it goes beyond simply using technology to enhance classroom delivery by potentially using purchased online courses delivered in the classroom or by engaging all students online while in the face-to-face environment.

Given that the demands of online teaching in K–12 are likely to be different from those in higher education due to the developmental level of students, the ways in which the courses are offered, the nature of the curriculum, and the need to be responsive to multiple audiences (students, parents, schools, districts, states, and even the federal government), what does it take to be an effective and even excellent online K–12 teacher? What specific skills do they need and what characterizes the excellent online teacher? An additional challenge not necessarily seen in higher education is that online teaching in K–12 is often used for what is known as "grade replacement" or "credit recovery." This refers to the ability for students to make up failing grades by participating in online instruction. Given this situation, a teacher may be faced with one or more unmotivated students or students who do not have sufficient skill with the subject matter being taught, thus creating significant need for additional tutoring, contact, and feedback to keep the students engaged and moving forward. Skills for dealing with unmotivated students need to be incorporated into teacher professional development for online teaching as a result.

CHARACTERISTICS OF EXCELLENT ONLINE TEACHERS

In Chapter Four, we reviewed the North American Council for Online Learning's proposed standards for K–12 online teachers. The National Education Association (NEA, n.d.) summarizes the characteristics of excellent online teachers as follows:

- Are prepared to use information, communication, course management systems, and learning tools and use them effectively
- Are motivated self-starters who can work well with minimal supervision
- Are student-centered and flexible
- Are focused on maintaining high standards
- Are able to promote and sustain online dialogue
- Are able to foster and sustain an online learning community
- Are able to facilitate collaborative learning
- Are able to collaborate with other teachers, support staff, and students to promote student success and participation online
- Are able to specify learning objectives and design authentic assessments to measure them
- Possess a sense of humor and can project their personality by developing an online voice (what is described in the online literature as the ability to establish presence)
- Communicate effectively in writing
- Have completed professional development courses and activities specifically geared to online teaching

Thinking back to the characteristics of excellence we presented in Chapters One and Two, it is clear that online teachers in K–12 education need to possess the same characteristics of excellence as their counterparts in higher education. There are differences, however. The first, and most obvious, is the need to be able to deliver developmentally appropriate education online. K–12 teachers learn not only to deliver subject matter, but also to deliver that subject at a particular grade level. Although this is true to some degree in higher education, it is not as much of an issue.

In addition, as the NEA points out, K–12 teachers must come into online teaching possessing all or most of these characteristics as they work in a very different system governed by certification requirements and state mandates. Much discussion is occurring in the K–12 world suggesting that teaching endorsements or professional certifications be earned prior to allowing a teacher to teach online courses (Deubel, 2008). This would require teachers to complete an unspecified amount of training in online teaching and then pass some sort of competency examination to determine whether or not they possess the skills necessary for online teaching. Deubel (2008) notes that four states currently have such certification requirements and that there is debate and discussion about the possibility of creating a national certification for online teaching. However, there is so much variability in the ways in which teachers are prepared to teach through their degree programs that unless some standardization of instruction occurs at the higher education level—something that is not likely to occur at any point in the near future—the ability to implement a national standard for online professional development becomes something of a pipedream or, at the very least, a continuing debate.

PRESERVICE TEACHER PREPARATION AND PROFESSIONAL DEVELOPMENT

Training and professional development in the K–12 sector occurs in three areas—professional development for veteran teachers who want to teach online and to meet continuing professional development requirements, preservice teacher preparation at the higher education level, and training for administrators who are tasked with evaluating teacher performance in online teaching. Let's now look at each of these areas individually.

Professional Development

A requirement for ongoing teacher certification is professional development. Consequently, it is not unusual for teachers to seek out opportunities to meet this requirement. Time, as mentioned earlier, can be a hindrance to successfully completing this requirement, however, and online training can be one way to address this (Fenton & Watkins, 2007). By participating in online training on a number of topics, teachers can gain the experience of being an online student while gaining deeper understanding of what online pedagogy requires.

Online classes aimed at preparing veteran teachers to teach online can also serve this dual purpose. The NEA (n.d.) suggests that an effective professional development program should reflect effective online pedagogy and delivery and that at least some of the training to teach online should occur online so as to "model the model" (p. 10). The NEA also suggests that given the 24/7 nature of online teaching, traditional professional development models that comprise after-school or one- or two-day face-to-face seminars are not particularly effective, thus making the online approach much more appealing for this population of teachers. Suggested topics for professional development include communicating online, providing feedback to students and parents, facilitating discussions and collaborative projects, using multimedia tools, and adapting curriculum for online delivery.

Many writers discussing professional development for online K–12 teachers also talk about the importance of mentoring. The use of master teachers to support the development of new teachers is a common practice in K–12 education and is considered to be particularly useful when learning to teach online.

Fenton and Watkins (2007) describe a partnership between a community college district and school districts to deliver online training. Their conclusion is that such partnerships serve two purposes: improving the level of preservice training for prospective teachers at the community college level and providing the online training needed by teachers in school districts. Such partnerships also have the potential to raise the bar in terms of instructional quality in both arenas.

Preservice Teacher Preparation

According to the NEA (n.d.), preservice teacher education has not traditionally included any requirements for studying online teaching and many programs still do not have such a requirement. They recommend that at a minimum, teacher education should include instruction on the following topics:

- The use of Internet resources, digital fluency, and digital literacy
- Fair use and copyright
- Identification of websites that support the work of teachers and that contain material that teachers can integrate into their work
- Issues of accessibility and disability compliance
- Acceptable use of technology and the Internet, along with Netiquette guidelines

- The development of lesson plans that integrate the use of the Internet for research

In addition, they recommend that preservice teachers take at least one online course on the pedagogy and practice of teaching online. That course should include

- Practice in both asynchronous and synchronous discussions, along with a critique of their use
- Instruction and practice in community building
- Practice and critique of the use of collaborative and team-building activities
- Creation and delivery of online lessons that can be critiqued by others in the class

Given that preservice teachers are required to complete student-teaching experiences before they graduate, the NEA suggests the inclusion of online student teaching in teacher education programs. This would involve learning and delivering course content each week under the supervision and mentoring of an experienced online teacher. In addition the student teacher could be involved in any professional development activities in online teaching offered by the school district.

Administrator Preparation

One of the challenges cited by the NEA (n.d.) in the development and delivery of online K–12 classes is the ability of administrators to evaluate online teachers in the same fashion as they evaluate those who teach in the face-to-face classroom. Often, peer and self-review are components of teacher evaluation; but those evaluations are often accompanied by administrative classroom visits for the purpose of observing and evaluating teacher performance. They state, "Administrators need to know how to review online course delivery, looking for and evaluating teachers' skills in developing online communities of learners, fostering online discussions and team activities, effectively using online course delivery tools like grading books and enrollment systems, creating an effective online voice and presence, providing adequate and frequent feedback to discussions and student work postings, modifying online course content to meet individual student needs, and effectively selecting and using appropriate online tools to support online instruction" (p. 12). Clearly, the expectations of excellent online K–12 teaching are huge, and administrators have an equally large task in terms of evaluating their effectiveness, particularly given that most administrators have not taken or taught an online class. Also, administrators are required to hire teachers with the appropriate training for online teaching, establish and support professional development programs in their districts and schools, including mentoring programs, and make decisions about technology acquisition and support.

As a result, administrators are in equal need of preparation and professional development to support their ability to carry out this task. Not only would it benefit them to participate in or teach an online course so as to understand what happens in online teaching, but they would also benefit from participation in networks that educate them about technologies in use and the development of long-term plans for technology development and integration. Such networks do exist and as budgets get tighter will probably be essential for the future of online K–12 education.

COPING EFFECTIVELY WITH THE ISSUES AND CHALLENGES OF K–12 ONLINE TEACHING

What is clear is that to close the wide but interrelated gap, a digital divide of sorts, between teacher preservice education and the delivery of effective online K–12 teaching, cooperation and collaboration needs to occur between the K–12 and higher education sectors. Partnerships between school districts and community college districts, such as the one described by Fenton and Watkins (2007), may be one solution as it not only benefits both sectors, but encourages them to evaluate their online teaching practice.

It is becoming increasingly critical that instructors in higher education effectively integrate the use of technology and online teaching into their practice in order to meet the needs of the digital natives who are graduating from high school, where online classes are becoming ubiquitous, and moving on to college. In order to complete the cycle and train effective teachers to go back into the K–12 system, online teaching must become a part of the curriculum and practice of schools of education. In addition, given that K–12 education is governed by state policy, administrators and policymakers can have some influence on teacher training and what is required both in terms of preservice education in order to teach and also ongoing professional development programs. Their understanding of the needs and demands of and competencies for online teaching also needs attention in order to close the gap and provide the support, financial and otherwise, needed to help move teachers toward excellence in online teaching.

KEY POINTS IN K–12 ONLINE TEACHING

- The demand for online classes in K–12 education is increasing dramatically, and with it a demand for teacher preparedness and excellence for teaching online.
- The gap between preservice teacher training in higher education and the demand for effective online teaching in K–12 education must be addressed through the provision of courses in schools of education that focus on online pedagogy.
- Student-teaching programs should include online teaching in the K–12 environment.
- Although the same characteristics of excellence exist for K–12 teachers, they have the additional responsibility to deliver subject matter at a developmentally appropriate grade level.
- Ongoing professional development programs are needed in school districts to help prepare veteran teachers for online teaching and to provide ongoing support to those engaged in online teaching.
- If online teaching for grade replacement or credit recovery is being used in a school district, teachers need additional training to assist them in dealing with students who have motivation problems or insufficient skills.
- Administrators are also in need of training to allow them to better understand the demands of and competencies required for online teaching so that they can evaluate teacher effectiveness and also plan for and support effective online programs.

BECOMING YOUR OWN FACULTY DEVELOPER

If you are a K–12 teacher or teacher educator, becoming skilled in online teaching is becoming a critical component of your teaching career. Consequently, it's important to take advantage of professional development opportunities that will allow you to do so. Most important, take an online class so as to experience online education from a student's perspective, experience models of, we hope, good online practice, and develop your own skills in online pedagogy. The NEA also recommends participation in a certificate program for online teaching, a list of which we provide in Appendix B, to help you develop the skills you need to teach online.

In addition, there are many good websites devoted to online teacher professional development. The most notable is Tapped In (www.tappedin.org), a professional development community of practice for K–12 teachers. PBS and Discovery Channel also offer several professional development opportunities for teachers through their websites, which also include resources that teachers can use in the delivery of their classes. In Appendix B, we include a listing of several websites to support K–12 teachers in their online work. They are numerous, and it would be impossible to include all of them; however, this will give you a sampling of what is available and guide you to other resources.

PART THREE Connecting the Dots: Faculty Development and Evaluation

Linking Training to Faculty Evaluation

J ust as good models for online faculty development are lacking, so are good models for evaluation of online faculty. Fink (2008) discusses the failings of the practice of faculty evaluation in most institutions. He asserts that feedback to faculty needs to support two important organizational needs: to motivate and enable faculty to know how well they are doing, and to engage them in continuous professional development. Rarely are these two important functions linked in faculty evaluation processes. He goes on to describe what he calls the Model of Good Teaching, which includes four dimensions: design of learning experiences, quality of student–teacher interactions, extent and quality of student learning, and the teacher's efforts to improve over time. He further asserts that what is needed are criteria and standards of excellence in each category so as to use the model to evaluate teaching effectiveness and link that to ongoing professional development needs. Clearly, these dimensions of good teaching apply equally to face-to-face and online learning situations, but may in fact be easier to evaluate in the online setting due to the ability to see and capture all of the interactions and outcomes in the online component of the course. DiStefano and Witt (2010) note that "the online environment provides unusually rich documentation of course design and delivery" (p. 412).

Using Fink's Model of Good Teaching as a guide, we discuss principles of faculty evaluation as they apply to excellent online teaching in this chapter, along with suggestions for conducting faculty evaluation, including peer review. We explore in depth the need to link training to evaluation and make suggestions for better ways to develop ongoing training based on evaluation.

ONLINE COURSE EVALUATION AND FACULTY EVALUATION

Roberts, Irani, Telg, and Lundy (2005) note that most courses in higher education institutions are evaluated by surveying student attitudes and reactions toward the course at its conclusion. We have often referred to Brookfield's (1995) assessment of the use of student questionnaires, as he states that traditional course evaluations rarely measure what we want them to measure. He describes course evaluations as "smile sheets," since they generally ask students to rate how much they liked or disliked the instructor and ask very little about the learning experience itself.

In a learner-focused online classroom with an excellent online instructor at the helm, course evaluations should not focus on whether or not the student liked the instructor, but whether the course provided an opportunity for learning through the quality of the learning experience designed, the quality of learner–instructor interaction, and whether the course supported the achievement of learning objectives. Angelo and Cross (1993) suggest that instructors ask themselves three questions when evaluating their own courses: What are the essential skills and knowledge I am trying to teach? How can I find out whether students are learning them? How can I help students learn better? Responses to these questions point directly to the outcomes developed for the course and look at how successful the course activities were in helping students master them.

Arbaugh (2000) suggests that the impact of the course management system in use affects the ability of the instructor to deliver a high-quality learning experience online. He believes that there are four general categories of factors that influence online learning and should thus be incorporated into evaluation of online courses:

- Perceived usefulness and ease of the course
- Flexibility for students and instructors
- Ease of and emphasis on interaction
- Experiences with engagement

How then does course evaluation fit with faculty evaluation, and how do both relate to ongoing faculty development for online teaching?

Faculty Evaluation

Asking students to reflect on instructor performance is only one source of evaluative material and should not be the sole element on which instructor evaluation is based. Given the number of factors influencing student satisfaction with a course—the technology in use, ease of access to materials, the ability to interact easily with peers as well as the instructor, and so on—simply asking students how well the instructor performed or whether the instructor was present and provided help with course activities does not provide an adequate basis for evaluation. Williams (2003) suggests that once instructor roles and competencies are established, online instructors adequately trained and evaluated, and training has occurred, then faculty evaluation can be geared to how well the individual faculty member has mastered those roles and competencies and what training is still needed. In our own experience of training online instructors through our Teaching in the Virtual Classroom program, we have found that online instructors believe that instructional design and course facilitation skills are the most important to successful course delivery. It is important to remember, however, that many instructors do not write or design the courses they teach. Clearly in these cases, the focus of evaluation needs to be on course delivery and facilitation for successful learning outcomes. We are also of the strong belief that training in facilitation skills must come *before* training in course design, something that many may view as counterintuitive. However, until a new instructor understands how a course should be delivered online, how will he or she be able to design effectively?

In our book *Assessing the Online Learner* (2009), we presented the following checklist of exemplary competencies derived from our experience of online teaching that can be used to evaluate instructor performance:

Course Facilitation

- Instructor has posted course requirements clearly stating that students are required to interact with each other and with the instructor, a designated time frame for the interaction is stated, directions for how to participate in the interaction, standards for the quality or expectations of the interaction are set, and the outcomes of those interactions are noted (i.e., students receive points or a grade for the interaction).

- Instructor has made clear effort to establish a learning community among students in the course through the use of introductions, bios, ice breaker activities, the creation of a social space or café area in the course, promotion of informal communication, appropriate use of humor, and other appropriate efforts to personalize and humanize the course.

- Students are required to respond to discussion questions about the content of each unit or somehow apply what was learned for all learning objectives in the unit. Multiple methods of interaction are available and utilized (i.e., discussion board, e-mail, chat, virtual classroom technology, etc.). The instructor responds to student postings strategically, allowing for extension and deepening of the exploration of content.

- Guidelines provided by the instructor at the start of the course state that the instructor will provide feedback within a designated time frame, a clear description of how the task of providing feedback will be accomplished (how will the student receive the feedback, e-mail, discussion board, etc.), and the specific types of feedback that will be submitted—example: feedback on assignments, on class participation, etc., and the instructor holds to those guidelines.

- Learning activities are developed that support instructor-to-student interaction (instructor participates in discussion with students via a discussion board or virtual chat room), student-to-content interaction (i.e., responses to discussion questions regarding the content), and student-to-student interaction, is promoted and supported, required as part of the course through collaborative projects, group assignments, discussion board, and/or virtual chat assignments.

- Assessment of student learning is established and is given in a time-period that supports the student's learning (soon after learning activities have taken place).

- Assessments are designed so that they are responsive to the needs of the individual learner (i.e., alternative measures may be taken for students with special needs; assessments are designed to reflect the student population and are varied enough that they meet the needs of diverse learning styles; assessments involve student choice).

- Students' achievement of stated learning outcomes is documented and provided to the students as feedback on their learning activities and assessments; informal as well as formal feedback is provided by the instructor to the student and encouraged from student to student.

- A rubric is used for all gradable activities that illustrates what achievement will look like and requires both student and instructor input.

- Instructor provides feedback to students based on the rubric along with comments pertinent to strengths and areas of need in student work.

- Instructor offers multiple opportunities for students to give feedback on course content, the technology in use, and uses the feedback to make course adjustments as necessary.

- All competencies are clearly stated and written using action verbs that promote higher-order thinking skills, and communicate what learners will be able to do as a result of the learning experience.
- All competencies are observable and measurable—the instructor and learner will be able to see a product and/or process upon completion of the learning experience and quality is measurable.
- All competencies clearly represent knowledge, skills, or attitudes/values that the learner would use in applying course knowledge to real-world situations.
- Course content, outcomes, practice, and assessment are consistent and the relationship between them is clear.
- Each assignment is aligned to module and course objectives and can be mapped accordingly.
- Outcomes are linked to program competencies or professional standards when applicable.
- Material is chunked, meaning that it is divided into appropriate categories, units, lessons, etc., and contains learning strategies that involve both recall and application.
- Lesson or unit design includes clear learning objectives, motivational techniques, application activities, including discussion questions, and assessments that align with the material and the objectives for the unit.
- In addition to overall expectations and directions, each activity or assignment clearly indicates what students need to do, how and where they should submit results, etc.
- Assessment methods are designed so as to measure progress toward program competencies and course outcomes and there is strong alignment between assessment and outcomes.
- Course resources are current and are fully accessible to all students. Instructions are available on the site instructing those with disabilities on how to access all course resources (pp. 128–130).

In Appendix C, we present these criteria in the form of a rubric that can be used for faculty evaluation. The criteria capture three of Fink's (2008) categories—design of learning experiences, quality of student/teacher interactions, extent and quality of student learning—and can be linked to individualized faculty development plans to measure the instructor's efforts to improve over time through training and other development activities. The following table adapts Fink's model and sources for information by linking these to the types of development activities that might be used for continuous performance improvement.

Table 7.1
Dimensions of Teaching Linked to Training and Development Activities

Dimension	Source of Information	Training and Development Activities
Design of courses	Course management system (CMS) Course syllabus	Training on effective course design and effective use of CMS Coaching and mentoring activities Peer discussions
Teacher/ student interactions	Use of discussion board Virtual classroom or chat sessions Feedback to students	Training on effective facilitation Coaching and mentoring activities Peer discussions
Quality of student learning	Student papers and assessments Student feedback regarding course experience	Training on effective assessment online Training on development of learning outcomes and link to assessments Coaching and mentoring activities Peer discussions
Instructor efforts to improve practice over time	Student feedback regarding course experiences Peer reviews Development plan	Regular revision of development plan Mentor assessments Add to or revise developmental network

Maintaining a training and development mindset when conducting faculty evaluation helps sustain Zachary's (2000) concept of a learning organization that integrates training, development, and mentoring throughout the organization.

Who Evaluates?

Another concern regarding faculty evaluation is who conducts the review. Tobin (2004) points out that many administrators who are called upon to evaluate online instructors have never taught online themselves. Consequently, the evaluation tends to be based on criteria that apply to traditional face-to-face delivery and tends to evaluate the wrong things when it comes to teaching online. The use of mentoring and peer reviews can help to reduce this concern if not eliminate it.

In a mentoring–peer review approach to faculty evaluation, once a novice or beginning instructor receives training in online facilitation and course design, he or she would be assigned a mentor, who may be the insider or master faculty member who taught the course and who would shadow the first course or courses taught by the new online instructor. The mentor would provide ongoing formative evaluation of the teaching approach by meeting with the mentee regularly to offer feedback and support. The mentor may be asked to provide an evaluation report at the conclusion of the first course taught. Institutions using this method do not often include peer reviews as part of administrative review of the instructor, but rather as part of ongoing faculty development, except when performance is being questioned. If there are performance concerns, shadowing and coaching would continue until they are resolved or it is determined that the instructor is not an appropriate candidate for ongoing online teaching. This approach also helps develop a cadre of experienced online instructors who can provide ongoing peer review of courses and develop into future mentors themselves. The goal becomes continuous quality improvement of courses and effectiveness of facilitation rather than "monitoring" faculty performance.

Peer Review

Keig and Waggoner (2004) state in their promotion of the use of peer review, "Informed peers are ideally suited to assess colleagues' course materials and evaluation of students' academic work" ("What Assessment Methods Should be Used by Faculty for the Purpose of Instructional Improvement," para. 3). The results of a peer review process, just as the results of a mentoring process, should include opportunities for faculty to improve their facilitation of online courses, learn how to teach more effectively, practice new skills and techniques, and get regular feedback and coaching from peers.

Keig and Waggoner advise that the results of peer review become a form of formative assessment that is placed alongside of administrative reviews, considered as part of the administrative review process, but not its total. They note that the focus of these reviews is developmental rather than judgmental. Reviews conducted for the purpose of promotion, compensation, and tenure rarely contain elements that can be utilized for the improvement of teaching. The goal of peer review, however, is simply that. As mentioned earlier, the results of the peer review are for the purpose of professional development and quality improvement. Integrating a peer review process into a mentoring program for online teaching simply makes sense and is a logical outgrowth of the mentoring process.

MANAGING AND EVALUATING FACULTY AT A DISTANCE

DiStefano and Witt (2010) state, "Dispersed faculty members require a broad rethinking of organizational leadership and administrative strategies as well as a significantly increased focus on clear and consistent communication" (p. 404). Administrators at traditional institutions sometimes mistakenly think that their online classes will be delivered solely by on-campus faculty, and, due to concerns about the ability to manage faculty at a distance, several institutions have implemented policies to that effect. However, the reality is that online distance learning classes are often taught by adjuncts at a distance and many nontraditional institutions largely employ both part-time and full-time faculty at a distance. In order to manage a largely adjunct faculty, many institutions have used a lead faculty approach, wherein a core faculty member on campus, or who is employed full time by the institution but may be at a distance as well, is responsible for supervising the work of adjuncts and part-time faculty. The lead faculty member is likely to be an insider or master faculty who may also be responsible for training adjuncts and acting as a mentor to them.

Harrington and Reasons (2005) note the challenges to effective evaluation of online courses and the faculty who teach them by posing the following questions:

- Since adjunct instructors frequently teach distance education courses, what is the institution's policy toward evaluations for part-time faculty? Is this policy the same for on-campus and distance education courses?

- Distance education requires that instructors employ teaching strategies mediated by technology so as to bridge the separation of student and instructor. Are instructors properly prepared to teach at a distance?

- Student evaluations typically figure into the promotion and tenure process. Has the academic dean or department chairperson specified evaluation expectations and rewards for faculty teaching distance education courses?

- Distance education courses may be the product of a team of professionals, including instructional designers, producer-directors, and technical specialists, working alongside faculty. Is the technology's effectiveness being assessed alongside the faculty member's teaching effectiveness (p. 7)?

The question that we add to this list is, How are these challenges factored into faculty development efforts?

Green, Alejandro, and Brown (2009), based on a study of factors that affect faculty decisions to teach online, concluded that all faculty regardless of status with the institution engage in online teaching because they are attracted to the flexible working conditions that online teaching affords. This is likely to mean that even on-campus faculty who are teaching online will spend more of their time at a distance from campus and have less direct contact with administrators. Given this scenario, how can administrators effectively manage, train, and evaluate faculty at a distance?

Our contention is that there are three elements that need to be built into the online distance learning program in order to facilitate effective faculty management and reduce potential faculty resistance in meeting program and university expectations:

- *Communication and community building.* As we have stated, being a faculty member at a distance can be a very lonely experience. Frequent, clear communication is therefore critical to faculty effectiveness and faculty management. We have already discussed the importance of creating a faculty community as part of any faculty development effort. Green, Alejandro, and Brown (2009) noted from their research that a motivator for adjunct online faculty was a sense of connection to the university or universities for which they teach. By paying close attention to communication and the development of a sense of community among online faculty, that sense of connection and loyalty can be built. The connection to peers and administrators can help improve faculty performance as expectations are conveyed and the need for additional support can be surfaced and addressed.

- *Training and mentoring.* We have already argued and established the importance of mentoring as an integral component of the training and faculty development process. One element we have not yet discussed, however, is the need to incorporate and train faculty on policies and expectations related to online teaching. Often, adjunct faculty at a distance find themselves being evaluated on expectations and policies that they know nothing about. Incorporating those into training and reinforcing them through the mentoring process ensures that there are no surprises and increases the likelihood that expectations will be met with little resistance.

- *Faculty support.* Oomen-Early and Murphy (2008) were interviewed regarding their research on the obstacles to faculty participation in online learning. A theme that emerged from their research was the overwhelming sense on the part of faculty that administrators lack understanding about what it takes to teach online in terms of time, workload, and effort expended. They suggest some solutions to this problem, including the need for administrators to participate in the online instructor training being offered at their institution, teach an online course, or both. They also suggest that administrators stay current with the literature on online teaching and learning to become knowledgeable about issues such as appropriate course enrollment, course development, and online faculty evaluation. Green, Alejandro, and Brown support this contention and note that the lack of institutional support and a lack of recognition for teaching efforts in this area are significant disincentives to teaching online.

What we conclude from all of this is that faculty will be motivated to teach online and engage in faculty development efforts to advance their work if they feel welcomed by the institution, wanted, needed, and supported. Faculty evaluation needs to be built on a solid understanding of online learning, what it takes to teach online, the competencies of excellent instructors in the online environment, and the impact of technology on teaching. Faculty can be encouraged to move from visitor status to the level of master faculty with appropriate levels of training, support, and mentoring. Administrators need training as well to understand the tasks involved with creating a solid faculty development effort for online teaching and to develop appropriate strategies for its evaluation.

KEY POINTS ON LINKING FACULTY DEVELOPMENT TO EVALUATION

- Expectations for faculty teaching online should be clear, included in training and mentoring programs, and fairly evaluated.

- Peer evaluation and administrative evaluation are separate functions that work alongside one another but are not the same process.

- Faculty evaluation for online teaching should be focused on models of good teaching practice and should be linked to further faculty development with a continuous quality improvement focus.

- Evaluation should be focused on the main activities involved in online teaching—course facilitation and course development.

- Faculty evaluation should not be geared toward excluding faculty who may not be performing up to par, but instead should focus on what they need to do to improve practice.

- Mentoring programs are an integral part of faculty evaluation and development and should be used to help coach faculty in areas of need.

- Managing faculty at a distance involves clear, consistent communication as well as the incorporation of training and mentoring programs and strong administrative support.

- Administrators should participate in training for online teaching, should teach an online course, or both in order to understand the demands involved and how online faculty can best be supported.

- A sense of connection to the institution along with a sense that the work of the online instructor is appreciated and understood are key factors in retaining online faculty.

BECOMING YOUR OWN FACULTY DEVELOPER

Even if there is no formal faculty development program at your institution, you can still engage in peer review of online courses through the peer network you identified at the end of the last chapter. Develop an agreement with one another about how you will engage in this activity. The agreement should include the criteria you will use in reviewing each other's courses and how you will share and use the resulting information.

In addition, you can engage in educating the administrators at your institution about the realities of online teaching and begin to discuss the importance of linking training to evaluation. Find and share articles that discuss various aspects of online teaching and faculty development—the reference list for this book is a good start. If you have the opportunity to create your own development plan as part of the evaluation process in your department, you'll be a step ahead. Finally, invite the administrators who are in charge of evaluating your teaching practice to "sit in" on your online course—set up a time to walk them through the various aspects of the course or courses you are teaching and explain what you are doing online. This type of education for administrators is invaluable and helps model for them what is involved in good course development and delivery.

Best Practices in the Development of Excellent Online Faculty

A survey conducted by Allen and Seaman (2007) revealed that more than two-thirds of higher education institutions in the United States are offering some form of online education. In addition, 69% of traditional and nontraditional universities believe that student demand for online courses will continue to grow. As of 2007, 83% of the institutions already offering online courses expected their enrollments in these courses to continue to increase. Based on this level of demand, it is clear that the need for experienced faculty to teach these classes is huge and that institutions need to develop plans for recruiting, hiring, training, developing, and supporting online faculty (Green, Alejandro, & Brown, 2009).

The final chapter in this book addresses this need by bringing together what we consider to be best practices in online faculty development. In so doing, we address first faculty developers and those faculty who are tasked with facilitating faculty development on their campuses, then faculty who are in charge of their own development, and finally administrators who are responsible for online distance education at their colleges and universities. Although many of these practices overlap, each group has particular needs and concerns that make up what Hagner (2001) refers to as "best systems," which comprise a "comprehensive and integrated package of support services and engagement practices" (p. 31). We contend that it is through a comprehensive, systems approach that the excellent online instructor will emerge.

BEST PRACTICES FOR FACULTY DEVELOPERS AND FACULTY TASKED WITH FACULTY DEVELOPMENT

Certainly, faculty developers and those tasked with coordinating this effort on campus need significant support from their institutions to carry out the job of training and developing faculty for online teaching. We address the institutional support concerns later in this chapter. However, apart from a focus on the institution, Green, Alejandro, and Brown (2009) suggest that those conducting faculty development should focus their efforts in three main areas: training for instructors at all experience levels, assistance with course development, and mentoring. We add a fourth dimension to this list, which is tailoring training to meet faculty needs. The following are ways in which each can be addressed.

Tailoring Training to Meet Faculty Needs

To begin any training effort focused on online teaching, two types of surveys should be delivered. The first should determine the level of experience each faculty member has with regard to online teaching, including the types of technology they regularly use. Once determination of faculty experience levels is established, then the second survey can be deployed; this survey should focus on what technologies faculty would like to know more about and what topics in the realm of online teaching would be most helpful to them. The results of these surveys will help in constructing a training program that most closely addresses felt needs and is likely to attract more faculty to attend and participate. More recently, institutions that have been conducting such surveys and have been asked to provide training experiences for faculty around those needs have contacted us. The topics they have asked us to deliver include how to maximize use of a discussion board, best practices in instructional design, how to maximize the hybrid environment, how to best make the transition to online teaching, and the like.

Training for Instructors at All Experience Levels

As we discussed at length earlier in this book, determining faculty experience levels and then developing and delivering training that is targeted at those levels is critical to the successful development of online faculty. Providing such training promotes faculty satisfaction with the online teaching process and results in better-developed and more successful online experiences for students. Vignare (2009) notes that faculty satisfaction is tied to two elements—choice and preparedness. If faculty are forced into the online environment, they are less likely to engage fully or design learning experiences that fit well online, whereas faculty who choose to teach online and who are given sufficient time, training, and support to do so are more satisfied with the outcome and simply do a better job of teaching online. We cannot stress enough that training works and is important to the development of excellent online instructors.

Best practices in faculty training also include the use of online training; instructors who experience what it's like to be an online student are more sensitive to student needs in terms of reasonable course loads, need for regular feedback and interaction, and a robust and engaging learning experience. The following is some anonymous feedback received at the close of a faculty training delivered online:

> I found this course to be an intensive online experience as my regular workload was increasing. I found myself working over-time in the normal workweek digesting information and responding to the academic content, as well as the personal contact, while trying to participate in the course to learn from my colleagues. I was able to experience firsthand a possible online experience for our new online education program at the college and to extrapolate, albeit slowly, some of the issues raised in the postings to my ever-changing workplace.
>
> Participating in a college committee involving faculty and administrators involved in online education, I felt I could give a student perspective [on] the institution's online education program. Personally, I was excited and pleased to learn some new technical skills. I found myself having new respect for these students as they work with me and I try to interpret the requirements, rules, [and] culture of this new medium with them.
>
> I enjoyed my experience with this online course. Although I was not able to participate in the discussion threads very much these last 2 weeks, I have learned from the experience. As I work with

students who are taking or planning to take an online class, I will be better able to advise them [regarding] time commitments, strong self-motivation, realistic expectations, etc. While I learned from the experience without necessarily jumping into every discussion, I'm not being graded.:-) The students do need to be concerned with what is expected of them in terms of participation. It has been enjoyable to begin learning about this new learning environment! Overwhelming. Confusing. And yet enlightening. I think I have learned that what sometimes may seem like a well-structured experience on my end may not be so from the perspective of my students. Ultimately, they as a group need to organize their environment in a way that makes most sense to them.

I have learned that online learning takes a lot of time, but I enjoy writing and reading the writing of others.... I've learned what it might feel like to be a new online student who was anxious about where and how to post assignments.

I realize if students are frustrated in the beginning of the class, it might affect their performance in the class.... I've also learned how important it is for online teachers to find other online teachers to share their teaching experiences with and the need for us to find, explore, update, and do research in this field.

The reflections of these instructors indicate that significant learning came out of their experience of being students online. The experience is likely to assist them in developing and facilitating courses that are more responsive to the needs of learners. They have seen what it is like on the "other side" of online learning. This is invaluable learning—learning that is difficult to convey in face-to-face training.

Assistance with Course Development

Teaching online is different from teaching face-to-face. Although all of our colleagues who write and present about online teaching echo this sentiment, there is still a pervading belief that all an instructor needs to do is to move what has been done in the face-to-face classroom to the online classroom with little to no modification. Even the most seasoned faculty in the face-to-face classroom, however, might not intuitively know how to build interactive courses online.

Current course management applications make it easy for faculty to simply transfer material to a course site. The lure to do this is complicated by the fact that institutions, which may view online distance learning as their lifesaver during times of on-campus declining enrollment, are now registering such large numbers of students in online classes that the burden on faculty is enormous. As a result, institutions are increasingly hiring faculty only as facilitators and leaving the responsibility for course development to a team that may or may not include the faculty member who will be teaching the course. Facilitating a team developed course is not necessarily a bad thing. Twigg (2003) recommends the development of master courses that are designed by a subject matter expert in conjunction with instructional designers and instructional technologists and that can be taught by any faculty member in the discipline. Doing so helps create scalable programs that can accommodate larger numbers of students over multiple sections.

Furthermore, the assistance of instructional designers and instructional technologists can help move faculty away from the desire to deliver a course using lecture as the primary means of instruction. When presented with instructional design principles that promote interactive delivery appropriate to online teaching, faculty will often ask, "Where is the lecture?" An appropriate response to this question is presented by Lytle, Lytle, Lenhart, and Skrotsky (1999), who state, "Lectures are important and certainly numerous in higher education, but are not necessarily any more valuable in the learning process than any other learning tool" (p. 58). Unfortunately, newer technologies have made the use of lecture easier to do online—lecture capture software allows an instructor to audio or videotape lectures that can easily be put into online courses. But does this represent best practices in online course design? Incorporated into faculty training and development, then, should be concrete ways in which content can be presented without the use of lectures. Some of the techniques can include the following:

- Creating Web pages that contain no more than one screen of text and graphics
- Collaborative small-group assignments, such as jigsaw assignments in which students contribute pieces to the whole of a topic or problem
- Research assignments asking students to seek out and present additional resources available on the Internet and in books and journals
- Simulations that mimic real-life work applications of the material discussed, such as asking a group to become a work team to develop a proposal on a given topic to be submitted to a fictitious company

- Asking students to become "experts" on a topic within the scope of the course and to then present that topic to their peers
- Asynchronous discussion of the topics within the scope of the course material being studied
- Fishbowl discussions whereby one group of students presents and discusses a topic while the other students observe, journal, reflect, and comment on their reflections at the end of the discussion
- Papers posted to the course site and peer reviewed
- Limited use of audio and video clips
- WebQuests, which are Internet-based scavenger hunts requiring that students find pieces of information related to a topic
- Use of Web2 technologies, such as wikis (collaboratively created web pages) and blogs (web logs or journals) to encourage collaborative completion of assignments (Palloff & Pratt, 2007)

What is important is to encourage and support faculty in thinking outside the box in terms of developing creative ways to present course content and to assess student performance, keeping in mind the technology to which students are likely to have access.

Mentoring

Green, Alejandro, and Brown (2009) support our model of mentoring for online teaching by suggesting that institutions implement a process whereby veteran faculty (or what we call insider or master faculty) serve as mentors to provide guidance and support on any number of issues important to online teaching. Included in this process is peer review whereby the mentor observes or shadows the newer online instructor to provide feedback and suggestions for continuous quality improvement. Because faculty developers cannot be all things to all faculty, including more experienced faculty in the training process incorporates a wider range of ideas while helping to foster a sense of community among all of the faculty who are teaching online at a given institution and across institutions. Sharing best practices in mentoring and community building with other institutions not only breaks down potentially competitive barriers, but also helps elevate the practice level across the discipline of online teaching. It also opens doors to additional research and a recognition that teaching online is, in fact, a discipline in and of itself.

BEST PRACTICES FOR FACULTY ENGAGED IN THEIR OWN DEVELOPMENT

Whether formal faculty training is offered at an institution or not, self-development is an important component of the movement toward excellence in online teaching and can be achieved in numerous ways. We have been providing suggestions for self-development at the conclusion of each chapter of this book. The recommendations for self-development fall into two major categories—self-assessment and the development of a training plan.

Self-Assessment

In order to take responsibility for their own learning, faculty should regularly assess their training needs and how best to meet them. That process includes determining what phase of development they are in, the general needs for that phase, and their own specific needs. Self-assessment for visitor and novice faculty should begin with a determination for readiness to teach online, while beginner, insider, and master faculty can seek out training that helps them move forward, furthering their skill in online teaching. One way to begin is to take an inventory of the types of technology the instructor is already using, including e-mail, word processing programs, and presentation programs such as PowerPoint. How often are these technologies being used, and how comfortable does the instructor feel in using them? Is more training needed in the use of basic technologies as a place to start?

Once a needs assessment has been conducted, faculty can then seek out resources on campus, at conferences, or online that address specific skill development for their disciplines or for online teaching in general. Reassessment on a regular basis is critical in the movement toward excellence—technologies change, teaching approaches change, and students change. Instructors must be able to stay abreast of these changes in order to be effective. The focus, however, should remain on acquisition of skills that will serve student learning outcomes—tying training to teaching is critical even when the instructor is seeking out his or her own resources.

Development of a Training Plan

Regardless of whether faculty training and development programs are available on campus or through the institution of which a faculty member is a part, each instructor should develop a training plan that incorporates the needs addressed in the self-assessment as well as any interests in the area of teaching with technology. For example, is the instructor interested in teaching in Second Life? Is there an interest in incorporating Web 2.0 technologies such as blogs and wikis into a course? What other technologies would help meet the learning objectives of the course and require exploration and training? Once the needs and interests are determined, training approaches and courses that address the needs and interests can be identified and those who can be helpful in the process can be contacted. All of this can be integrated into a flexible training plan that changes as needs and interests change. Please see Appendix A for an example of and template for such a plan.

An important component of a training plan is the creation of a developmental network, which includes peers and colleagues who can help with certain types of skill development or simply be available for consultation. In addition, informal networks of faculty working to develop online courses can meet regularly to share concerns and progress and offer support to one another. Collaborative approaches to self-development also result in the emergence and maintenance of a faculty learning community, which is particularly important for adjunct faculty or those teaching at a distance. This serves not only to support skill and practice in online teaching but also to reduce the isolation that often occurs when teaching online while maintaining a connection to the institution.

A formal or informal mentoring program is also an important component of the training plan. Mentoring programs can be run by the institution using faculty who are at the insider or master level of online teaching or can be informal, emerging out of developmental networks or those identified by the individual faculty member as having particular skills that would be helpful to his or her development in online teaching.

The components of a training plan, then, should minimally include

- Identification of needs and interests
- Determination of what individuals, groups, or training courses or programs can meet those needs
- Creation of a developmental network to address individualized needs
- Informal networks of faculty engaged in online teaching
- Formal or informal mentoring

What is most important is developing the plan, assessing it regularly, and modifying as needed. By empowering faculty to take charge of their training needs, and developing a plan that is flexible and aimed toward continuous quality improvement, excellence can be achieved, even if no formal training is provided on campus.

BEST PRACTICES FOR INSTITUTIONS

Good planning of online programs, including how online offerings fit within the curriculum and concomitant need for faculty, is critical to success. Green, Alejandro, and Brown (2009) provide advice to institutions for the development and support of online faculty. Their suggestions involve providing fair compensation for online teaching, particularly taking into account the increased workload involved with course development and dissemination. Given that adjunct faculty often work for several institutions, they recommend issuing multiterm or multiyear contracts to adjuncts to help develop loyalty to the institution. Finally, they recommend that institutions evaluate where the teaching of online courses fits with tenure and promotion—something that is often an issue at many institutions.

How do these suggested practices relate to the development of excellent online faculty? By paying attention to these important issues, institutions convey that they value the faculty who teach online, value the impact of online courses in the curriculum, and value the functions of training and support as these appear to be the motivators for faculty who teach online.

However, paying attention to these issues also means budgeting for these issues. A survey regarding faculty development needs conducted at The Pennsylvania State University (Taylor & McQuiggan, 2008) revealed that the preferred learning modes for their faculty predominantly favored one-to-one approaches with a mentor or colleague, instructional designer, or technical staff over face-to-face sessions on campus. Online resources including reference material posted online, self-paced training modules, and instructor-led training modules fared better than did face-to-face sessions. Faculty preferred more informal or self-paced, self-directed forms of development to formal events. Another interesting finding was that faculty did not value extrinsic rewards for online course development and teaching, such as release time or rewards in the form of additional pay or certificates. Instead, what they said would motivate them to develop online courses and teach online is the availability of training along with resources and individualized support. Although this is one study at one campus, these findings support our observations about faculty who teach online, why they do so, and what would encourage them to continue. Planning and budgeting, then, needs to utilize this information, and resources for faculty development for online teaching needs to be more responsive to what it is that faculty want and need—perhaps less emphasis can be placed on large, formal training events and more focus instead on hiring support personnel. The authors of the Penn State study concluded that professional development needs for online faculty are a moving target—likely to change as our knowledge of online teaching grows and technology changes. However, one thing is certain: providing support for faculty is likely to keep them engaged in online teaching and move them in the direction of excellence.

Hagner (2001) notes that the development of an institutional culture that embraces technology and online teaching is dependent on three critical determinants: leadership, inclusion, and communication. He describes the leadership needed as "courageous leadership" (p. 31) that is willing to strive for consensus by investing time, resources, and support aimed at overcoming the challenges of moving toward an increasing online presence for the institution. A sense of inclusion, as we have been discussing, is crucial to the success of any online endeavor—faculty need to feel valued and their voices heard in the development plan for online teaching and learning. Voices that should also be included in the process are those of students and staff—a systems approach includes all who are creating, supporting, and receiving online courses and programs. As important as inclusion is the element of communication—about the online program itself, policies and procedures, changes in policy, challenges and successes. Inclusion and communication are important elements of community, and the creation of community should be a value that undergirds this effort.

A "BEST SYSTEM" FOR DEVELOPING EXCELLENT ONLINE INSTRUCTORS

When faculty are provided with good training and support for online teaching and learning, the likely outcome is excitement about the new ways technology can impact teaching and learning. There is enthusiasm about the meeting of learning objectives in deep and meaningful ways. When courses are designed and delivered with interactivity in mind, a shift occurs as learners become more empowered and discover that the learning in an online course comes from other students and not solely from interaction with the instructor. Ways in which students can collaborate with one another are built into courses, and more authentic means of assessing student performance accompany those activities. Self-reflection and critical thinking become important components of assessment. In fact, when courses progress well, the instructor often learns as much from his or her students about online teaching as students learn from the instructor about the content. The reflection of one of our students at the end of an online course demonstrates this shift:

> I wanted to take another opportunity to thank each of you for your participation in this course. I remember when I first joined the program . . . [other students] talked about the importance [that] their colleagues played in their success in the program. I had no idea of the significance of those statements, or the degree to which they were true, until I experienced it for myself. Thank you all for this tremendous contribution to my development.

This reflection is the type we hope to see at the end of a course. It gives us an indication that the planning and delivery of the course was effective not only in achieving learning objectives but also in moving students toward what we consider to be real learning—the cocreation of meaning and knowledge.

It is a systems approach to online faculty development that moves faculty toward excellence and results in positive student feedback on their online course experiences. According to Hagner (2001), the best systems for online faculty development are "comprehensive and integrated package[s] of support services and engagement practices" (p. 31). When best practices in the areas of faculty development, self-development, and institutional support are integrated into one comprehensive system, the overlap between the three results in the outcomes we hope to see from these efforts—community, continuous quality improvement, faculty leadership, support, and overall online program excellence. Figure 8.1 illustrates the "best system" we envision.

When instructors and students are able to reap the benefits of a well-designed online course or program, the end result is excitement about what is possible

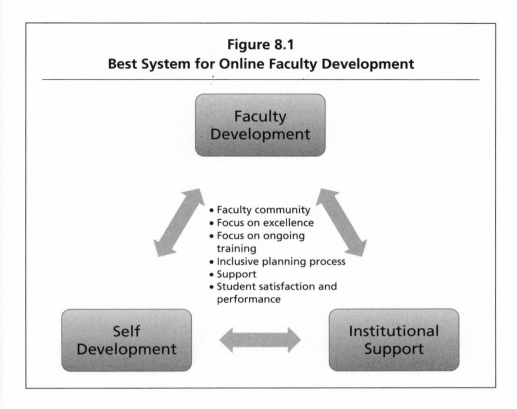

Figure 8.1
Best System for Online Faculty Development

Faculty Development

- Faculty community
- Focus on excellence
- Focus on ongoing training
- Inclusive planning process
- Support
- Student satisfaction and performance

Self Development

Institutional Support

in the online realm and about the new relationships that are developed between instructor and student, among students, among faculty, and across institutions. The resultant excitement about learning helps stimulate new creative approaches to online teaching and demonstrates that there can be and is, in fact, an excellent online instructor.

Resources for Faculty Developers, Faculty, and Administrators

While planning for and writing this book, it became clear to us that we are addressing three, sometimes distinct, audiences—those engaged in faculty development activities who may be faculty members themselves, faculty who are seeking resources for their own training and development, and administrators who are charged with running online distance learning programs and evaluating the faculty who teach within them. Given the different needs of each group, we include resources to support the work of each.

Appendix A is directed toward faculty developers and faculty who are coordinating faculty development activities on campus. Faculty who are involved in their own training and development are also likely to gain from the resources contained in this appendix. Appendix B is a listing of resources to support faculty in several areas: communities of practice, online training, online conferences, and online journals. Appendix C is directed toward administrators and contains resources to support their work in the area of faculty evaluation.

Some of the resources we present are of our own design. Other resources have either been donated to us by colleagues or are adaptations of the work of others. We have given credit to those who have contributed to our ongoing learning and are grateful to them for the work they are doing in service of the discipline of online teaching and for students.

Resources for Faculty Developers and Those Tasked with Faculty Development

Contained in this appendix are resources to support the work of faculty developers or those tasked with coordinating faculty development efforts on their campuses. The resources include

- Faculty training plan
- Sample training syllabus for a basic online training for novice and beginner faculty
- Sample training outline for a two-part advanced training

INDIVIDUAL FACULTY TRAINING PLAN

An Assessment of Faculty Readiness to Teach Online can be found in Appendix B. This assessment can also be used by faculty developers to enable them to develop training that corresponds to the level of development of individual faculty. The following charts can be used to help faculty determine their individual training needs and who they identify to help them meet those needs in the form of a developmental network. The samples provided are for a novice faculty member who is interested in teaching online and has need to develop basic skills. It can be assumed, based on this plan, that the novice instructor showed greatest need in online teaching skills, followed by technical skills. Time management and the instructor's attitude toward online teaching are areas of strength. This does not mean that these areas should be excluded from attention in the training plan, but they will not need as much emphasis.

This instructor is at the line between a novice and apprentice instructor. Strengths are openness to online teaching and time management skills. This

Category	Skill Level (based on self-assessment)	Areas of Need	Plan to Meet Training Needs
Technical skills	28—has basic computer and word processing skills	CMS skills Discussion facilitation Use of virtual classroom software	Participation in 6-week online training for online teaching, including use of CMS, facilitation skills, and use of Elluminate.
Online teaching experience	8—Has had no online experience to date	Experience online environment from both student and teacher perspective	Participation in online training should address this need. Training should include ability to deliver lesson from instructor role. Follow-up mentoring support will be needed.
Attitude toward online teaching	27—Is open to online teaching experience but will need help in instructional delivery	Means of instruction beyond lecture Discussion facilitation Design and delivery of collaborative activities	Online training to start followed by mentoring support. Mentor should shadow first online class for ongoing feedback.
Time management and time commitment	27—Area of strength	No real needs in this area. Continue to support in maintaining good time management approach	Mentor support

Total score = 90 points.

instructor will need significant support in the development of technical skills and pedagogical skills for online teaching.

[*Note:* Please refer to Chapter Two in this book for more specific training suggestions for each phase of instructor development.]

DEVELOPMENTAL NETWORK FOR NOVICE FACULTY

The following is the developmental network for the novice faculty member whose needs were described in the training plan above.

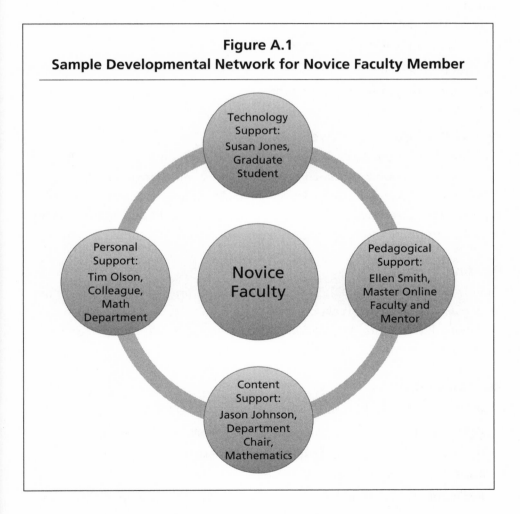

Figure A.1
Sample Developmental Network for Novice Faculty Member

Technology Support: Susan Jones, Graduate Student

Personal Support: Tim Olson, Colleague, Math Department

Novice Faculty

Pedagogical Support: Ellen Smith, Master Online Faculty and Mentor

Content Support: Jason Johnson, Department Chair, Mathematics

SAMPLE TRAINING SYLLABUS FOR NOVICE OR BEGINNER FACULTY

The following is a basic training syllabus that we have used for online delivery of new faculty training. The syllabus can be modified in terms of length of time required for training and can also be modified to add or delete topics. As presented, this represents a four-week training.

INTRODUCTION TO AND BEST PRACTICES IN ONLINE TEACHING

Instructors
Rena M. Palloff PhD
E-mail: rpalloff@mindspring.com

Keith Pratt PhD
E-mail: drkpratt@mindspring.com

Course Description and Overview

This course is designed as a four-week online orientation to online teaching. It will focus on developing a shared vocabulary of technical language and will discuss the pedagogical concerns in delivery of quality online education. In addition, focus will be on creating online courses that lead to desired learning outcomes by effectively blending course content with appropriate use of technological tools.

Reading

Palloff, R., & Pratt, K. (2003). *The virtual student: A profile and guide to working with online learners.* San Francisco: Jossey-Bass.

Palloff, R., & Pratt, K. (2005). *Collaborating online: Learning together in community.* San Francisco: Jossey-Bass.

Prerequisites
- No prior coursework in online teaching and learning is required.
- Basic computer and word processing skills, such as copy and paste, etc.
- Participants need basic understanding of the use of e-mail and the ability to access the course site and other sites on the Internet.
- Review of course texts is strongly recommended prior to beginning this course.

Learning Outcomes

- Experience an online course from the perspective of the learner
- Explore and integrate various online teaching and learning strategies
- Explore and integrate the concept of learning communities in online teaching
- Begin planning for the development of the faculty member's own online course
- Apply the concepts of good course development to a course that can be immediately implemented and delivered
- Be able to critique the positive elements in courses developed by others as well as make appropriate suggestions for improvement
- Integrate good assessment techniques into an online course

Learning Units
Week 1

Unit 1 Intros, learning objectives, guidelines (three days).

Unit Overview This unit is designed to help us get to know one another and to discuss how we will work together online. It will help get you to become more familiar with your course management system as we navigate it together, post our introductions, review learning objectives for the course, and discuss guidelines for participation. The following are a few guidelines for participation in this course:

- Given the short duration of the course (4 weeks), you are expected to log on almost daily.
- You are expected to post to the discussion at least once per unit and in response to one of your colleagues at least once.
- All assignments should be completed on time so as not to hold up progress in the course.
- All communication will be professional and will observe the rules of Netiquette. For more information about Netiquette, visit www.albion.com/netiquette.

Unit Objectives

- Meet one another
- Develop a contract for learning during this course

Assignments

- Post an introduction to the discussion board in the appropriate discussion forum. Include not only information about your background, but also your experience with online teaching and learning. Reflect on the following questions in your introduction: What drew you to teach online? How do you see yourself as an instructor? What are your hopes and fears about beginning your online teaching experience?
- Respond to at least one other person's introduction.
- Post a message to the discussion board indicating your willingness to work within the guidelines listed in the overview for this unit. Are there any guidelines that should be added?

Unit 2   Syllabus development in online learning (three days).

Unit Overview   The syllabus forms the backbone of any course and, in the online course, is critically important as it is the main way that students gain understanding of what is expected of them in the online classroom. Consequently, very little can be left to assumption in the syllabus for the online course. As online instructors develop syllabi, there is a need to leave behind what has been done in the face-to-face classroom and to rethink the course for online delivery. There are several questions they need to ask themselves in order to do so. They are as follows:

- Who are my students?
- What do I want to accomplish through this course? What do I want my students to know, feel, or do as a result of this course? What course content will support these objectives?
- What guidelines, rules, roles, and rituals need to be established for this course?
- How do I plan to deliver course material?
- How comfortable do I feel including collaborative activity, personal interaction, promoting knowledge acquisition by learners, and releasing control of the learning process?
- How do I want to organize my course site?
- How will I assess student performance?
- How will I address attendance requirements?
- What do I want to see students walk away with when they conclude this class?

In addition to answering these questions, online instructors need to consider new and different activities to access course content. Read-and-discuss online courses are not engaging and may lead to poor participation down the line. Consequently, thinking out of the box is strongly encouraged!

Unit Objectives

- Develop a stronger understanding of the nature of online learning
- Consider new ways to deliver course material

Assignments

- Review the textbooks for this course and then post answers to the following discussion questions in the appropriate forum on the discussion board: What ideas do you have for presenting course material? What activities might you try? What concerns do you have about the questions to consider listed in the unit overview and how might you address them?

Week 2

Unit 3   Choosing appropriate learning activities (three days).

Unit Overview   Now that you are more familiar with your course management system, the purpose of this unit will be to help you choose and more fully develop activities for your class. Chapter 11 in *The Virtual Student* (Palloff & Pratt, 2003) discusses best practices in online learning, including understanding who students are and how they learn, as well as what they need to support them in their learning. *Collaborating Online* (Palloff & Pratt, 2005) offers a number of suggestions for engaging the online learner in collaborative activities. With these as a guide, you will revisit your prospective learning activities and more fully develop them for implementation in your own course.

Unit Objectives

- More fully develop a set of learning activities for implementation in an online course
- Explore the concept of engagement and how to integrate that into a course

Assignments

- Review Chapter 11 in Palloff and Pratt and the entire book, *Collaborating Online*. Given these materials as a backdrop, how can you more fully develop the activities you suggested in Unit 2? What makes these effective activities and how will they tie into your learning objectives for your course? Which tools will you use to deliver these activities and why?

- Post answers to these questions in the appropriate discussion forum on the discussion board.

- How do you view the concept of engagement? How will you ensure that your students are fully engaged in your course? Please post your answers to the appropriate discussion forum and respond to at least one other colleague.

Unit 4   Promoting participation (three days).

Unit Overview   Effective delivery of an online course demands high participation on the part of students and instructors. You have been developing ideas for your course, but if you cannot get students to participate, your efforts have been for naught. The following are some suggestions to maximize participation (Palloff & Pratt, 1999):

- Be clear about how much time the course will require of students and faculty in order to eliminate potential misunderstandings about course demands—include this information in your syllabus.

- Teach students about online learning—include a "Frequently Asked Questions" area of your course as well as a place where students can ask you questions as they arise.

- As the instructor, be a good model of participation by logging on frequently and contributing to discussions—plan to participate as often as you ask your students to participate.

- Be willing to step in and set limits if participation wanes or if the conversation is headed in the wrong direction.

- Remember that there are people attached to the words on the screen. Be willing to contact students who are not participating and invite them in.

- Create a warm and inviting atmosphere that promotes the development of a sense of community among the participants.

Keeping these points in mind can help to maximize participation and create a satisfactory learning experience for both students and faculty.

Assignments

- Review the sample participation guidelines presented in *The Virtual Student* on pp. 145–146. Present the guidelines you intend to use in your online course in the appropriate forum on the discussion board and provide feedback to at least one other colleague on their set of guidelines.

- Review the sample faculty expectations in *The Virtual Student* on pp. 146–150. Write a welcome letter to your students and post it on the discussion board. Provide feedback to at least one other colleague on his or her letter.

Week 3

Unit 5   Collaboration and reflection (three days).

Unit Overview   In the online environment, collaboration is seen as the cornerstone of the educational experience. Collaboration forms the foundation of a learning community while bringing students together to support learning and promoting creativity and critical thinking. In addition, collaboration creates an environment of reflection—students, while engaged in collaborative work, are required to reflect on the process as well as the content being explored. The result is a transformative learning experience—the student no longer views the content in the same way. Social interaction, rather than individual exploration, expands students' view of the topic and what they thought they knew. It allows them to question previously held beliefs and explore new ones. In addition, the use of collaborative activity in a class helps address issues of learning style and culture, allowing students to work from their areas of strength. Collaboration helps our students become more than just students—it allows them to become reflective practitioners. It is important to remember, however, that collaboration does not just happen. The instructor plays a critical role in preparing students for collaborative work. The stages for collaboration are as follows:

- Set the stage

- Create the environment

- Model the process

- Evaluate the process

Think about the collaborative activity you may be planning for your online course with these phases in mind. How might you facilitate the collaborative process?

Unit Objectives

- Plan for collaborative work in an online course
- Create activities that promote reflection and transformative learning

Assignments

- Review once more the activities that you are proposing for your online course and answer the following question in the appropriate forum on the discussion board—what might you do to incorporate collaborative work in your online course? If you have already planned for collaborative activity, how do you plan to get students ready for that activity? How might you need to prepare them? Post your plan and provide feedback to at least one other plan.

- Answer the following on the discussion board: How will you promote reflection in your course? Will this be a graded activity?

Unit 6   Incorporating evaluation (three days).

Unit Overview   Assessment of student performance is a critical component of any class, be it face-to-face or online. As we learned from reading Chapter 8 in *The Virtual Student,* good assessment aligns with teaching activities and is not seen as an added burden by either the student or the instructor. Angelo and Cross (1993) note that good assessment is based on the following factors and is

- Learner-centered
- Teacher-directed
- Mutually beneficial
- Formative
- Context-specific
- Ongoing

In this unit, we will spend more time thinking about critical assessment and evaluation activities in your online course.

Unit Objectives
- Develop appropriate assessment activities for the online course
- Prepare and present a grading rubric for assessments

Assignments
- Review Chapter 8 in *The Virtual Student* and also look at the assessment activities presented in *Collaborating Online.* Post the following to the appropriate forum on the discussion board: What assessment activities are you preparing for your online course? Discuss how they align with course objectives and learning activities. Give at least one colleague feedback on his or her proposed assessments.

- Prepare and post to the discussion board at least one draft of a grading rubric for one of the learning activities in your course. Provide feedback to at least one colleague on his or her rubric.

Week 4

Unit 7   Prepare a lesson (four days).

Unit Overview   You are now at the point where you are ready to begin creating your course! During the next few days, you will be expected to pull one learning unit together in draft form and present it for review.

Unit Objectives
- Complete a draft of one learning unit of your course, including all learning and assessment activities
- Give and receive critical feedback for lesson improvement

Assignments
- Present the draft lesson with activities and assessments and/or rubrics to your colleagues. Provide a critique to at least one colleague.

Unit 8   Final reflections on the learning experience (two days).

Unit Overview   Congratulations! You made it through this very intensive training experience! Now that you have, it's time to take a deep breath and reflect a bit on what you've learned over the last four weeks. Think about how you will approach your online course, your students, and what you might yet need to help you with your development as an online instructor.

Unit Objectives
- Critically reflect on the training experience
- Define areas that need further work and final questions

Assignments
- Respond to the following questions in the appropriate forum on the discussion board: What new learning have I gained from participating in this training? How might I do things differently in my online class than I might have without the training? What unanswered questions do I still have?

ADVANCED TRAINING OUTLINE

George Engel, doctoral student at Walden University and calculus instructor in New York, submitted the following award-winning advanced training seminar outline on the topics of mobile computing and the use of wikis. George uses both together in his math classes.

FACULTY TRAINING ON THE USE OF MOBILE DEVICES COMBINED WITH WEB 2.0 TECHNOLOGY

Instructor
George Engel (engel.george.b@gmail.com)

Day 1 (Four Hours)—Day Theme: The Mobile Classroom
I. Introduction and biography of speaker

II. Why mobile devices? (PowerPoint)

A. What is the classroom we want? (picture of laptops at every desk)

B. Reality of classroom we have (picture of empty desks, no tech)

C. Why technology has not fully integrated
- Not enough resources
- Not enough planning time
- Out of date equipment
- Technical issues

D. Limitations

- Learners find the technology immobile
- No impact outside the classroom

E. Mobile devices are the solution (cell phones and Ipod touches)

III. Divide group into cooperative groups of three to four with a heterogeneous grouping of curricular groups. These will be the breakout groups for the day.

First Activity: The Audience Response System (ARS)

- Group warm up with Wiffiti.com.

- Have groups get to know each other by completing activity using Wiffiti.com and their cell phones as research tools. This activity is included at the end of this syllabus.

- This activity should take approximately 30 minutes. Expect to have to train participants on how to submit text-based message responses.

- Intro PowerPoint on ARS.

  Examples: be sure to show actual examples where needed.

  > Senteo

  > Polleverywhere.com

  > Wiffiti.com

  Benefits

  > Anonymity

  > Participation

  > Engagement

  Activities

  > KWL

  > Do Now (Warm up)

  > "Exit Polling"

  > Check for understanding

- Polleverywhere.com question

  How could an audience response system be used in your subject area?

Show website and options for polleverywhere.com and demonstrate how to set up various polls with group.

Have a polleverywhere.com poll active that participants can submit questions to throughout the day.

Second Activity: Flickr.com Time

• Show student examples of flickr slide shows from student-generated wiki.

• Have participants create a flickr account and demonstrate to them how to upload a picture from their phone. (This may require an elmo, if available.) Have each group choose a topic from the following list: Sports, nature, mechanics, mathematics, technology, language, art, and diversity. Begin next activity. This is located at the end of the syllabus. (Be sure to have collected cell phone numbers before the activity, so participants can be texted an alert of when to return.)

• This activity should take at least 60 to 90 minutes to complete.

• PowerPoint on other examples

The Flip Book (show examples of student work)

Museum journeys (students take pictures at a museum and then comment on each one)

Travel journal for a field trip

• Allow time for discussion about the merits of this activity. This is extremely important for the group to process what they have learned and observed in the activity.

Third Activity: Lights, Camera, Action!

• In this activity, participants will create a two- to three-minute video with their phones that explains how to use flickr.com to create a slide show.

• Power Point: Show various video streaming sites and give benefits and drawbacks of each

YouTube

Blocked by many districts

Rapid upload and approval of content

Directly upload from a phone

TeacherTube

    Not blocked

    Poor upload and approval times

    Directly upload from phone

Google Video

    Blocked by many districts

    Rapid upload and approval of content

    Directly upload from a phone

Hpgabbel.com

    Not blocked

    Easy upload

- Benefits to learning (this needs to be developed)

- Give participants time to develop and upload videos. Once done have the group view all videos

- After this, discuss this activity and how it might apply to their lessons. Give them time to process and ask questions about work.

Wrap Up and Conclusions   Spend time discussing the day's work and have the group state what they have enjoyed and learned. Also, answer questions that have been submitted on polleverywhere.com.

Homework   To prepare for next session, write down three questions that you still have about what we have been doing.

Day 2 (Two Hours)—Day Theme: Web 2.0 Technologies
Open with Review of Homework   Spend time answering questions that they may have developed over night.

Activity One: Wiki Time

- What is a wiki? Spend time discussing what a wiki is and how many have used it.

- Project time. Break people into common curricular groups.

- Show each group how to create a wiki. Have them log into wikispaces and create an account for their group. Let them practice each of these. Have videos and pictures prepared for them.

  Editing and adding pages

  Adding photos and text

  Embedding slideshows and videos

- Show examples of student created-wikis.

- The groups will begin the "Wiki Creation Project."

  Project examples:

  Scientific catalogue

  Poetry collection

  Geometric shapes

  Civil War wiki

- When the project is complete, have each group view all the wikis and make comments on the pages by using the discussion option of the wiki. As they comment have them think of how they would like their students to comment.

- Group discussion on the process. Answer any questions. Ask them how they may use them in the classroom. Also, ask other ways they might use a wiki for learning.

Final Activity: What Is Web 2.0?

- Have participants complete the "What is Web 2.0?" activity.

- Complete the activity.

- Have each group present ideas to class. Have someone recording the various ideas. Discuss how they may use these technologies in their classrooms.

- Print all of this information for the groups to take with them.

Conclusions and Final Discussion of the Lessons

- Wrap up the session with a discussion of what they have learned over the two sessions. Answer any final questions. Leave them with this thought. "How are they going to put what they have learned here to use? Are they going to continue teaching in the twentieth century? Or are they going to move into the twenty-first?"

• Upload all materials that the group created to Google Docs so that they may use and share the material.

Student Activities Included in the Training
The following are the descriptions of how to use the student activities described in the training.

Ten-Minute Activity

• Group members will use their cell phones to find and answer the questions included in the directions for each group.

• The purpose of this activity is to introduce the participants to two ideas:

1. What invention is credited to Dr. Martin Cooper? Txt @wif18506 + your answer to the number 87884	2. Who is responsible for the invention of Peanut Butter? Txt @wif18508 + your answer to the number 87884
3. What is the most famous Constitution Class Star Ship? Txt @wif18509 + your answer to the number 87884	4. In what country did the mathematical matrix first appear in recorded text? Txt @wif18511 + your answer to the number 87884

The use of wiffiti.com

The use of mobile devices for Internet research.

• Students respond well to this activity and enjoy the process. A second type of activity of the same nature:

Group A
Answer the following questions, texting all responses using: @wif9923 + your message to 87884.

(Each group member should send one answer.)

1. What is a polynomial?

2. What is the minimum number of terms required to form a polynomial?

3. Name three operations that are allowed between two polynomials.

Group B

Answer the following questions, texting all responses using: Text @wif9970 + your message to 87884.

1. Name five types of math or sciences that use polynomials.

Group C

Answer the following questions, texting all responses using: Text @wif9972 + your message to 87884.

1. Name four people known to have contributed to the mathematics of polynomials.

Group D

Answer the following questions, texting all responses using: Text @wif9973 + your message to 87884.

(Each group member should send one answer.)

1. What is the degree of a polynomial?

2. What is the name of a fourth, fifth, seventh, and tenth degree polynomial?

A Flickr.com Activity   Each group will choose from the following list of topics or choose one of their own that must be approved by the instructor at the beginning of the activity.

Sports

Mechanics

Nature

Mathematics

Technology

Language

Arts

Science

Diversity

Culture

History

Each group will roam the campus for at least 30 minutes taking pictures that represent their chosen theme. At the end of the allotted time, the participants will return to the presentation room and upload their photos to flickr.com. Once all photos are uploaded, participants will create a slide show using flickr. They should then prepare an explanation of why each slide is indicative of their theme. One group member will present the slideshow to the class, giving the explanation for each slide.

The purpose of this activity is not just to teach how to use a web service like flickr but to introduce participants to possibilities of the use of such a service.

"Wiki Creation Project"

• Your group will create a wiki that fits your curricular area. You may use the suggested themes of Scientific Catalog, Poetry Collection, Geometric Shapes, Civil War, or any theme that they wish to work with as long as it is in their curriculum.

• Your group is to create five different pages to your wiki. Each page should fit the following criteria:

1. Home page: This should be a colorful page with pictures that describe the content of the wiki.

2. All remaining pages should reflect the content of the following:

   One item from your theme, i.e., poem, Civil War general, etc.

   There should be a complete description of the item along with pictures and even supporting videos for the content. This description should be in your own words.

• The pages should show good content, be pleasing to the eye, and easily read. Be sure to indicate where information has been received and create hyperlinks for any content that has come from the web.

Web 2.0

1. As a group, define web 2.0 technology.

2. Spend the next 30 minutes researching the Internet to find three web 2.0 tools that could be used for learning. Be sure to

   a. Describe each tool

   b. State how it might be used in their classes

   c. How it might be used in other curricula

3. Prepare a presentation or you definition and tools that you have found.

4. Present the information to the class.

Appendix B: Resources for Faculty

This appendix contains resources for faculty to support their own training and development. Included are links to and suggestions for

- Assessment of faculty readiness to teach online
- Communities of practice
- Certificate programs in online teaching
- Online conferences
- Online journals
- Professional organizations
- Course evaluation rubrics

ASSESSMENT OF FACULTY READINESS TO TEACH ONLINE

Just as there are numerous online tools to assess student readiness for online learning, a number of tools for assessing faculty readiness to teach online are emerging. Two online resources for such tools are Online Learning.net sponsored by UCLA (http://www.onlinelearning.net/InstructorCommunity/selfevaluation.html) and one developed collaboratively by the Pennsylvania State University and the University of Central Florida (2008) (http://weblearning.psu.edu/news/faculty-self-assessment/). The assessment we present is an adaptation of both along with our own added questions to address teaching philosophy and pedagogy.

Although lower scores on this assessment are an indicator that more training and support are necessary to be successful in online teaching, the instructor should be encouraged to pursue training if interest exists. Training can be targeted to the areas of greatest need and should be an indicator of how an individualized training plan can be developed. The areas of the assessment are scored on a 1-to-5 scale with total scores for each section, and then the ratings within each are used to determine the areas of emphasis for the individualized training plan, as shown in the sample Individual Faculty Training Plan in Appendix A. The total scores are an indicator of the phase of development in which the instructor finds himself or herself, allowing for the creation of an individualized training plan to meet the needs at that phase. For more description of the phases, please refer to Chapter Two in this book.

	1 = Strongly Disagree	2 = Disagree	3 = Neither Agree nor Disagree	4 = Agree	5 = Strongly Agree
1. Technical Skills—Total possible points = 60					
I have a computer available to me at home and/or in my office					
I travel with a computer					
I access the Internet frequently and can search the Internet for what I need					
I am competent in using e-mail					
I am competent in using word processing software					
I am competent in using presentation software such as PowerPoint					
I am able to download files from the Internet and can attach files to an e-mail					
I am familiar with and can create a blog					
I am familiar with and can create wikis					
I am familiar with and can use social networking technologies, such as Facebook and Twitter					

	1 = Strongly Disagree	2 = Disagree	3 = Neither Agree nor Disagree	4 = Agree	5 = Strongly Agree
I am familiar with my university's course management system					
I have used technology to support my face-to-face teaching					
Total Points:					

2. Experience with Online Teaching and Learning—Total possible points = 40

I have experienced at least one online course as a student					
I have received training in online instruction					
I have used online quizzes in teaching my classes					
I have used online discussions in teaching my classes					
I have used virtual classroom tools like Elluminate, Adobe Connect, WebEx, or Skype in teaching my classes					
I have used chat in teaching my classes					
I have used a publisher website in teaching my classes					
I have used my university's course management system to supplement my classroom teaching					
Total Points:					

3. Attitudes Toward Online Learning—Total possible points = 45

I believe that online learning is as rigorous as classroom instruction					
I believe that high-quality learning experiences can occur without interacting with students face-to-face					

(Continued)

	1 = Strongly Disagree	2 = Disagree	3 = Neither Agree nor Disagree	4 = Agree	5 = Strongly Agree
I support the use of discussion as a means of teaching					
I support learner-to-learner interaction and collaborative activity as a central means of teaching					
I recognize that community-building is an important component of online teaching					
I encourage students to bring life experiences into the classroom and create activities that draw on those experiences					
I believe that lecture is the best way to convey content in my discipline					
I feel comfortable communicating online and feel that I am able to convey who I am in writing					
I am a critical thinker and can develop assignments that encourage critical thinking in my students					
Total Points:					

4. Time Management and Time Commitment—Total possible points = 30

I am able to log in to an online course at least once a day					
I am able to post to my online class at least 4 to 5 times per week					
I am able to manage my time well					
I am flexible in dealing with student needs on such issues as due dates, absences, and make-up assignments					

	1 = Strongly Disagree	2 = Disagree	3 = Neither Agree nor Disagree	4 = Agree	5 = Strongly Agree
I am fairly organized and tend to plan ahead in my teaching					
I am responsive to my students, responding to e-mail within 48 hours and assignments within one week					
Total Points:					
Total Points for All Sections:					

Interpretation of Results

150–175 points = You are well suited to online teaching and are probably an insider or master online instructor.

90–150 points = You are likely to need some support for success in online teaching and are probably an apprentice online instructor.

Below 90 points = You will need considerable training and support for success in teaching online and are probably a visitor or a novice online instructor.

[*Note:* For more explanation of the training needs of each phase of online instructor development, please refer to Chapter Two and also to the sample training plan in Appendix A.]

COMMUNITIES OF PRACTICE

The following is a sampling of communities of practice devoted to online teaching.

Learning Times [http://www.learningtimes.net]

Learning Times is a host for online communities, training, and conferences on topics in online and distance learning.

Merlot (Multimedia Educational Resource for Learning and Online Teaching) [http://www.merlot.org]

Merlot is a repository of learning objects and also produces an online journal and hosts discipline-specific communities of practice.

Tapped In [http://tappedin.org/tappedin/]

Tapped In is a community of practice primarily geared toward K–12 teaching but has been expanding its focus to include higher education faculty.

CERTIFICATE PROGRAMS IN ONLINE TEACHING

Numerous certificate programs exist in the area of online teaching. The following is a sampling of the best known. Some offer graduate level credit along with certification.

Fielding Graduate University—Teaching in the Virtual Classroom Graduate Certificate Program [http://www.fielding.edu/programs/elc/tvcC/default.aspx]

The Teaching in the Virtual Classroom (TVC) academic certificate program goes beyond use of the technological tools to delve deeply into the pedagogy of online teaching and learning and building learning communities therein. This two-semester program is delivered completely online and credits can articulate into Fielding's doctoral program in Educational Leadership and Change. Program directors and faculty are Rena Palloff and Keith Pratt.

University of Wisconsin-Stout—E-Learning and Online Teaching Graduate Certificate [http://www.uwstout.edu/soe/profdev/elearningcertificate.html]

Designed to meet professional development goals to be certified as highly qualified in the area of e-learning instruction and online training. Students can take one or two courses per term. The program is five semesters long if one course is taken or nine months if two courses are taken per term. Courses can count toward elective credit in three master's degree programs in education.

LERN (Learning Resources Network) Certified Online Instructor (COI) Program [http://www.teachingonthenet.org/courses/certified_online_instructor/index.cfm]

The Certified Online Instructor designation has been created to serve faculty in higher education and others teaching online who want to gain recognition for their knowledge and skills. The COI program involves taking three core one-week intensive courses, teaching two courses online, having a course critiqued, gathering student evaluations of the online courses taught, and taking an exam.

University of Wisconsin-Madison Extension Division—Professional Certificate in Online Teaching [http://www.uwex.edu/disted/depd/cert_benefits.cfm]

> Flexible, self-paced certificate program that focuses on helping new online instructors get up to speed quickly or reinforces and advances skills of experienced online instructors. The program provides knowledge and skills, examples, and best practices in online teaching through opportunity to practice and demonstrate what has been learned in a course planning project that uses the instructor's own course materials.

Illinois Online Network Master Online Teacher Certificate [http://www.ion.uillinois.edu/courses/students/mot.asp]

> The Master Online Teacher certificate is a comprehensive faculty development program based upon the MVCR (Making the Virtual Classroom a Reality) series of online faculty development courses. This program recognizes and certifies faculty, staff, and administrators who achieve a measurable level of knowledge related to online course design, online instruction, and other issues related to online teaching and learning. In order to earn the Master Online Teaching certificate, a student must successfully complete four core courses, one elective course, and the online teaching practicum.

ONLINE CONFERENCES

Online conferences are growing more popular due to economic constraints associated with travel and registration fees and the convenience of participating from one's home or office. Some extend over two or three days whereas others are brief seminars. The additional benefit of online conferences is their low cost.

Jossey-Bass Online Teaching and Learning Conference

http://www.onlineteachingandlearning.com/

International Online Conference

http://www.internationalonlineconference.org/

Smithsonian Conference on Problem Solving

   http://www.smithsonianconference.org/expert/

Fielding Graduate University Online Summer Institute for Community Colleges (OSICC)

   www.onlinefacultyinstitute.org

TCC (Technology, Colleges, and Community) Online Conference

   http://tcc.kcc.hawaii.edu/2010/tcc/welcome.html

Academic Impressions

   http://www.academicimpressions.com/

Magna Online Seminars

   http://www.magnapubs.com/calendar/index-cat-type.html

ONLINE JOURNALS ABOUT ONLINE TEACHING

There are numerous journals currently online. This is a list of some that are devoted to the topic of online teaching.

Journal of Online Learning and Teaching (JOLT)

   http://jolt.merlot.org/

Online Journal of Distance Learning Administration

   http://www.westga.edu/~distance/ojdla/

T.H.E. Journal (Transforming Education Through Technology)

   http://thejournal.com/articles/2004/09/01/faculty-training-for-online-teaching.aspx

EDUCAUSE Review

   http://thejournal.com/articles/2004/09/01/faculty-training-for-online-teaching.aspx

Innovate: Journal of Online Education

   http://innovateonline.info/

Journal of Asynchronous Learning Networks (JALN)

   http://www.sloanconsortium.org/publications/jaln_main

Journal of Interactive Online Learning

http://www.ncolr.org/

The International Review of Research in Open and Distance Learning

http://www.irrodl.org/index.php/irrodl/index

International Journal of Instructional Technology & Distance Learning

http://www.itdl.org/index.htm

The Technology Source Archives

http://www.technologysource.org/

PROFESSIONAL ORGANIZATIONS

The following is a partial list of professional organizations of interest to faculty teaching online and to faculty developers:

ISTE—International Society for Technology in Education

This organization is dedicated to supporting the use of technology in the teaching and learning of K–12 teachers and students.

AACE—Association for the Advancement of Computing in Education

This organization's mission is to advance Information Technology in Education and E-Learning research, as well as its development and practical application.

USDLA—United States Distance Learning Association

This organization promotes the development and application of distance learning for education and training at all levels.

League for Innovation in the Community College

The League supports the work and publications focusing on the integration of technology in teaching.

AACC—American Association of Community Colleges

Although not directly focused on the use of technology in education, AACC provides resources and research for and about community colleges.

POD Network—Professional Organizational Development Network

Provides resources and support for faculty developers.

NCSPOD—The North American Council for Staff, Program, and Organizational Development

Provides resources and support for faculty developers.

COURSE EVALUATION RUBRICS

Several institutions and organizations have created rubrics for the evaluation of quality in an online course. They can be downloaded and used to evaluate one's own course or can be used as part of a course evaluation effort at the department or institutional level. The best known of these are

Quality Matters

http://www.qualitymatters.org/

California State University-Chico Rubric for Online Instruction (ROI)

http://www.csuchico.edu/celt/roi/

Illinois Online Network—Quality Online Course Initiative Rubric

http://www.ion.uillinois.edu/initiatives/qoci/rubric.asp

Appendix C: Resources for Administrators of Online Programs

Contained in this appendix are resources for administrators of online programs and those who are responsible for the training and evaluation of online faculty. Included are

- Training needs assessment for online programs
- Faculty self-evaluation questions
- Sample faculty evaluation rubric

TRAINING NEEDS ASSESSMENT FOR ONLINE PROGRAMS

The following is a template that can be used in the development of a strategic plan for online learning. Working through it will help provide a start to the development of an inclusive and comprehensive foundation to support online learning. It is designed to explore the development of a strategic plan in which the implementation of technology in teaching plays a prominent role; investment in the technology infrastructure needed to support such an effort; support by senior leadership for the use of technology; faculty support for those who engage in the use of technology in their teaching; and support for students through access to computers, courses, and the Internet.

General Issues and Concerns

What evidence is there that this program is needed? What problems would this program address or resolve? If no information is currently available, how will we obtain this information?

How will we know this program is successful?

Who should be involved in a planning effort on my campus to determine program design, technology acquisition and course development? What departments or areas should be represented?

Name:

Department/area:

Who will take charge of the planning effort?

How will decisions be made?

What approval mechanisms will be used?

Who are the students we anticipate we will attract? Why should they be attracted to this program at this institution?

Student groups:

Motivation to enroll:

Once a program is in place, how do we anticipate attracting/recruiting students?

Course and Program Issues and Concerns

How do we envision using technology? Will we consider it to be a support to the face-to-face classroom or will it be used to deliver classes and programs or both?

How will technology meet instructional needs in our institution?

What do we see as the implications of technology use in our institution?

How extensive do we anticipate the use of technology will be? Will its use be phased in or will we move directly to offering full programs that require immediate implementation?

What programmatic, course, and learning outcomes are we attempting to achieve?

How will the use of technology assist us in achieving these outcomes?

Investment in the Technology Infrastructure

What institutional support exists for the development of online courses and programs?

What kind of technology budget, in terms of money and time, can we expect to develop?

Will the institution support expenditure for technology on an annual basis? If so, what will it look like?

What technology do we already have in place?

What do we need to acquire?

What hardware and software do potential learners have access to? Is that compatible with the program's potential demands? What will we need to provide on campus?

What do we anticipate the setup costs for new equipment, materials, development, and personnel to be? [*Note:* The following website can be very helpful in determining costs of a potential online program regardless of size: http://webpages.marshall.edu/~morgan16/onlinecosts]

Will we offer stipends or release time to faculty for course development? If so, how much?

How will we offer training to faculty and students? Will we need to outsource training or can it be done in-house? What will it cost and how will it be accomplished?

What do we intend to charge for tuition for online courses?

Faculty Support and Training

How many faculty are interested in and ready to teach online classes?

Who are they?

How many faculty will we need to train so that they can begin to develop and teach online classes?

What levels of training do we need to provide—from novice to experienced users?

How do we intend to provide training for faculty? What will it cost us to deliver training on an ongoing basis?

How will we support faculty in the development of online courses? Will we use a team approach including instructional designers and instructional technologists?

Will we be able to offer faculty incentives for course development? If so, what will they be?

Will faculty be expected to teach online courses in addition to their existing teaching loads or will they be light-loaded in order to teach online?

How will we provide ongoing faculty support once classes are up and running?

Student Support

What are student training needs? How will we meet them?

What will it cost us to train our students?

What additional support will we offer students who are taking online classes?

How will students link to other campus services such as registration, records, bookstore, and library services?

Will we charge students a technology fee? Will students be expected to pay the same fees as campus-based students?

How will we provide technical support to both faculty and students?

How will students be evaluated in terms of learning outcomes established for online courses and programs? How will the courseware selected assist us in the evaluation of students and the achievement of learning outcomes?

Policy Issues and Concerns

Do we have an existing policy on intellectual property? If not, how will we develop one and what will it entail?

Do we have an existing policy on course and program approval? If so, how will it apply to online courses and programs?

How will we amend faculty contracts in order to include the development and teaching of online courses?

SELF-EVALUATION QUESTIONS FOR FACULTY

The following self-evaluation questions are an adaptation of those presented as a "practice evaluator" by Beetham and Sharpe (2007). These questions can be used as part of a faculty evaluation process to allow reflection on their own online teaching practice and can be used to evaluate one online unit of a course or an entire teaching/learning experience. Questions are both descriptive and reflective.

Descriptive Questions

1. What learning outcomes did you establish for your learners?
   - Did they meet the outcomes?
   - How well do you think they were able to achieve the outcomes?
   - What activities did you use to achieve outcomes?
   - Were there choices of activities involved? If so, was there a pattern to their choices and what was that pattern?

2. Did your learning activities promote interaction among learners?
   - Were they able to work collaboratively with one another?
   - Did they engage in social interaction in addition to interaction around assignments?
   - How extensive or robust would you say discussion was in the course?
   - Was the majority of interaction learner-to-learner or was it primarily directed to you as the instructor?

3. Did learners bring additional resources into the course?
   - What resources did they access and use?
   - Were the resources that they found and shared useful and relevant?
   - What percentage of learners engaged in seeking out additional resources?
   - Did you expect and promote this activity?

4. What technologies did your learners use?
   - Did they primarily use the course management system or did learners use other technologies such as chat, virtual classroom applications, blogging, or wikis?
   - Were all learners able to access and use the technology for the course?
   - Were there any technical issues that emerged?
   - Was the use of technology advantageous or a challenge in the learning process?
   - Was the technology in use and the technical support provided adequate for your course?

5. Was feedback adequate in the course?

- Did learners engage in sufficient learner-to-learner feedback?
- How quickly and how often did you provide feedback?
- Did learners feel that they received enough feedback from you?

Reflective Questions

1. What was the learning experience like for learners?

- Did they meet expected learning outcomes?
- Did they seem to enjoy the class and the learning experience?
- Were students motivated and involved throughout?
- Were there any surprises or unexpected benefits to students?
- What informal feedback did you receive along the way?

2. What was the learning experience like for you as the instructor?

- Were there challenges? If so, how did you meet them?
- Did you feel supported in your teaching experience by staff and colleagues?
- Did you enjoy the teaching experience?
- Did your work online allow you to express your preferred teaching style, values, and beliefs about learning?
- Did you develop some new approaches?
- What worked well?
- What would you do differently next time?
- What advice would you give to a colleague who was about to teach the same online course that you taught?
- What advice would you give to a colleague who was about to develop an online course?

FACULTY EVALUATION RUBRIC

In our book, *Assessing the Online Learner* (Palloff & Pratt, 2009), we presented a rubric for evaluation of the level of interactivity in an online course. The rubric is equally useful in the evaluation of online faculty performance and the design of the online course. The following are categories through which interactivity and the course itself can be evaluated. The points can then be totaled and used as part of a faculty self-assessment or administrative assessment of the effectiveness of the course and faculty performance.

Scale	Development of Social Presence	Instructional Design for Interaction	Evidence of Learner Engagement	Evidence of Instructor Engagement
Low (1)	No attempts made—no intros, bios, use of collaboration. No presence of a café area in the course.	Students communicate only with instructor via e-mail. Content presented in "lecture" format through text and graphics. No use of discussion board and no required interaction between learners.	Learners respond to instructor as required but do not respond to one another.	Instructor responds to learner assignments but does not promote additional discussion.
Minimum (2)	Intros and bios are required.	Minimal use of discussion board but discussion is required—students are asked to choose discussion questions to respond to or discussion assignments occur at intervals rather than weekly.	Learners respond to discussion questions and, as required, to other learners. There is little evidence of voluntary discussion outside of assignments.	Instructor posts an expectation of timely feedback to learners, responds to learner assignments, and is present on the discussion board. Instructor may respond to every post, limiting student-to-student engagement.

(continued)

Scale	Development of Social Presence	Instructional Design for Interaction	Evidence of Learner Engagement	Evidence of Instructor Engagement
Average (3)	Intros and bios are required. An ice-breaker activity is included at the start of a course.	Discussion is a regular part of the course. Students are required to respond to discussion questions and to at least one or two peers weekly. Discussion may or may not be assessed.	Learners respond to discussion questions and provide minimum required feedback to peers that demonstrates application of course concepts. Some voluntary discussion beyond assignments is present with indicators that a learning community has formed.	Instructor posts an expectation of timely feedback to learners, responds to learner assignments and demonstrates some ability to promote learner-to-learner discussion through strategic response that summarizes or links student posts to extend discussion. Instructor shows some ability to develop a learning community.

Scale	Development of Social Presence	Instructional Design for Interaction	Evidence of Learner Engagement	Evidence of Instructor Engagement
Above Average (4)	Intros and bios are required. Instructor responds to intros and bios as a model for students. An ice-breaker activity is included at the start of a course and a café area is included in the course.	Discussion is a regular part of the course. Students are required to respond to discussion questions and at least two of their peers weekly. Dyad or small-group assignments are included in the course design. Discussion is part of the assessment scheme for the course.	Learners respond to discussion questions and to their peers and initiate discussion that goes beyond the assignments. Learner postings are substantive, show application of course concepts, and indicate engagement with course material and one another. There are indicators that a learning community has formed.	Instructor posts clear expectations of response to learner e-mails and assignments within a designated time frame, demonstrates good ability to promote learner-to-learner discussion through strategic response to discussions, and offers additional materials for consideration. Instructor shows ability to develop and maintain a learning community.

(continued)

Scale	Development of Social Presence	Instructional Design for Interaction	Evidence of Learner Engagement	Evidence of Instructor Engagement
High (5)	Intros and bios are required. Instructor responds to intros and bios as a model for students and may use audio or video as part of the instructor intro. An ice-breaker activity is included at the start of a course. A café area is included in the course and students are encouraged to engage with one another and the instructor in the café through informal discussion.	Discussion is a regular part of the course and is assessed. Students are required to respond to discussion questions and at least two of their peers weekly. Dyad or small-group assignments are included in the course design. The use of synchronous discussion media may be included.	Learners respond to discussion questions and to their peers and initiate discussion that goes beyond the assignments. Learner postings are substantive, show application and evaluation of course concepts, and indicate engagement with course material and one another. Learners engage in informal communications through the café area of the course and show strong connection to one another and the presence of a learning community.	Instructor posts clear expectations of response to learner e-mails and assignments, responds to learner e-mails within 24 to 48 hours and to assignments within 7 days, demonstrates good ability to promote learner-to-learner discussion through strategic response to discussions, and offers additional materials for consideration. Instructor shows good ability to develop and maintain a learning community.

Points to determine level of interactivity: Low, 1 to 8; Average, 9 to 15; High, 16 to 20.

REFERENCES

Akridge, J., DeMay, L., Braunlich, L., Collura, M., & Sheahan, M. (2002). Retaining adult learners in a high-stress distance education learning environment: The Purdue University executive MBA in agribusiness. *Motivating & Educating Adult Learners Online*. Essex Junction, VT: GetEducated.com.

Allen, I. E., & Seaman, J. (2007). *Online nation: Five years of growth in online learning*. Babson Survey Research Group: The Sloan Consortium.

Angelo, T. A., & Cross, K. P. (1993). *Classroom assessment techniques: A handbook for college teachers* (2nd ed.). San Francisco: Jossey-Bass.

Arbaugh, J. B. (2000). How classroom environment and student engagement affect learning in internet-based MBA courses. *Business Communication Quarterly*, *63*(4), 9–26.

Aycock, A., Garnham, C., & Kaleta, R. (2002). Lessons learned from the hybrid course project. *Teaching with Technology Today*, *8*(6), March 20. Retrieved from [http://www.uwsa.edu/ttt/articles/garnham2.htm].

Barker, A. (2003). Faculty development for teaching online: Educational and technological issues. *Journal of Continuing Education in Nursing*, Nov./Dec. 2003, *34*(6), 273.

Barlett, P. F., & Rappoport, A. (2009). Long-term impacts of faculty development programs: The experience of Teli and Piedmont. *College Teaching*, *57*(2), Spring 2009, 73–82.

Bates, A. W. (2000). *Managing technological change*. San Francisco: Jossey-Bass.

Beetham, H., and Sharpe, R. (2007). *Rethinking pedagogy for a digital age: Designing and delivering*. New York: Routledge.

Beldarrain, Y. (2006). Distance education trends: Integrating new technologies to foster student interaction and collaboration. *Distance Education*, *27*(2), 139–153.

Benor, D. E. (n.d.). Successful models of faculty development institutional/organizational approach. Retrieved from [www.academicpeds.org/education/nutsandbolts/pdfs/benor.pdf].

159

Boice, R. (1992). *The new faculty member: Supporting and fostering professional development*. San Francisco: Jossey-Bass.

Boulay, R. A., & Fulford, C. P. (2009). Technology mentoring: Research results across seven campuses. In A. Tatnall & A. Jones (Eds.), *Education Technology for a Better World*. Boston: Springer.

Bright, S. (2008). E-teachers collaborating: Process based professional development for e-teaching. Proceedings of ASCILITE 2008, Melbourne, Australia. Retrieved from [http://www.ascilite.org.au/conferences/melbourne08/procs/bright.pdf].

Brook, C., & Oliver, R. (2003). Online learning communities: Investigating a design framework. *Australian Journal of Educational Technology, 19*(2), 139–160.

Brookfield, S. (1995). *Becoming a critically reflective teacher*. San Francisco: Jossey-Bass.

Caffarella, R. (2002). *Planning programs for adult learners*. San Francisco: Jossey-Bass.

Carr-Chellman, A., & Duchastel, P. (2001). The ideal online course. *Library Trends, 50*(1), 16.

Chaney, B. H., Eddy, J. M., Dorman, S. M., Glessner, L., Green, B. L., & Lara-Alecio, R. (2007). Development of an instrument to assess student opinions of the quality of distance education courses. *American Journal of Distance Education, 21*(3), 145–164.

Charalambos, V., Michalinos, Z., & Chamberlain, R. (2004). The design of online learning communities: Critical issues. *Educational Media International, 41*(2), 135–143.

Chickering, A. W., & Gamson, Z. F. (1987). Seven principles for good practice in undergraduate education. *AAHE Bulletin, 39*(7), 3–6.

Chuang, H., Thompson, A., & Schmidt, D. (2003). Faculty technology mentoring programs: Major trends in the literature. *Journal of Computing in Teacher Education, 18*(1), 26–31.

Clay, M. (1999). Faculty attitudes toward distance education at the State University of West Georgia. *University of West Georgia Distance Learning Report,* December. Retrieved from [http://www.westga.edu/~distance/attitudes.html].

Cravener, P. (1998). A psychosocial systems approach to faculty development programs. *The Technology Source Archives*, November 1998. Retrieved from [http://technology source.org/article/psychosocial_systems_approach_to_faculty_development_programs/].

Deubel, P. (2008). K–12 online teaching endorsements: Are they needed? *T.H.E. Journal*, January 10, 2008. Retrieved from [http://thejournal.com/articles/2008/01/10/k12-online-teaching-endorsements-are-they-needed.aspx].

DiPietro, M., Ferdig, R. E., Black, E. W., & Preston, M. (2008). Best practices in teaching K–12 online: Lessons learned from Michigan virtual school teachers. *Journal of Interactive Online Learning, 7*(1), Spring. Retrieved from [http://ncolr.org/jiol].

DiStefano, A., & Witt, J. (2010). Leadership and management of online learning environments in universities. In K. E. Rudestam & J. Schoenholtz-Read (Eds.), *Handbook of online learning* (2nd ed.). Los Angeles: Sage.

Faculty Focus (2008). Overcoming obstacles to faculty participation in distance education. *Academic Leader*, March 2008.

Fenton, C., & Watkins, B. W. (2007). Online professional development for K–12 educators: Benefits for school districts with applications for community college faculty professional development. *Community College Journal of Research and Practice*, *31*, 531–533.

Fink, L. D. (2008). Evaluating teaching: A new approach to an old problem. In D. R. Robertson & L. B. Nilson (Eds.), *To Improve the Academy: Resources for Faculty, Instructional, and Organizational Development*, *26*, 3–21. San Francisco: Jossey-Bass.

Garrison, D., Anderson, T., & Archer, W. (2003). A theory of critical inquiry in online distance education. In M. G. Moore & W. G. Anderson (Eds.), *Handbook of Distance Education* (pp. 113–127). Mahwah, NJ: Lawrence Erlbaum Associates.

Gaytan, J., & McEwen, B. (2007). Effective online instructional and assessment strategies. *The American Journal of Distance Education*, *21*(3), 117–132.

Generation www.Y (n.d.). *Exemplary program*. Retrieved from [http://genyes.com/programs/genyes/research].

Goodyear, M. (2006). Mentoring: A learning collaboration. *EduCause Quarterly*, *29*(4). Retrieved from [http://www.educause.edu/EDUCAUSE+Quarterly/EDUCAUSE QuarterlyMagazine/MentoringALearningCollaboratio/157429].

Graham, C., Kursat, C., Byung-Ro, L., Craner, J., & Duffy. T. M. (2001). Seven principles of effective teaching: A practical lens for evaluating online courses, *The Technology Source* (Mar./Apr. 2001). Retrieved from: [http://ts.mivu.org/default.asp?show=article&id=839].

Gray, T., & Birch, J. (2008). Team mentoring: An alternative way to mentor new faculty. In D. R. Robertson & L. B. Nilson (Eds.), *To Improve the Academy: Resources for Faculty, Instructional, and Organizational Development*, *26*, 230–241. San Francisco: Jossey-Bass.

Green, T., Alejandro, J., & Brown, A. H. (2009). The retention of experienced faculty in online distance education programs: Understanding factors that impact their involvement. *International Review of Research in Open and Distance Learning*, *10*(3), 1–15.

Gunawardena, C. (1995). Social presence theory and implications for interaction and collaborative learning in computer conferencing. *International Journal of Educational Telecommunications*, *1*(2–3), 147–166.

Gunawardena, C. N., Ortegano-Layne, L., Carabajal, K., Frechette, C., Lindemann, K., & Jennings, B. (2006). New model, new strategies: Instructional design for building online wisdom communities. *Distance Education*, *27*(2), 217–232. Retrieved from [WiscomPub7_26_06[1].pdf].

Gunawardena, C. N., & Zittle, F. (1997). Social presence as a predictor of satisfaction within a computer mediated conferencing environment. *American Journal of Distance Education*, *11*(3), 8–25.

Hagner, P. R. (2001). Interesting practices and best systems in faculty engagement and support. *NLII White Paper, Final Report January 25, 2001*. Seattle: NLII Focus Session.

Hara, N., & Kling, K. (2000). *Students' distress with a web-based distance learning course: an ethnographic study of participants' experiences*. CSI Working Paper, Spring 2000. Retrieved from [https://scholarworks.iu.edu/dspace/bitstream/handle/2022/1092/wp00–01B.html?sequence=1].

Harrington, C. F., & Reasons, S. G. (2005). Online student evaluations of teaching for distance education: A perfect match? *The Journal of Educators Online*, *2*(1), January. Retrieved from [http://www.thejeo.com/ReasonsFinal.pdf].

Hawkes, M. (2006). Linguistic discourse variables as indicators of reflective online interaction. *The American Journal of Distance Education*, *20*(4), 231–244.

Hebert, M. (2006). Staying the course: A study in online student satisfaction and retention. *Online Journal of Distance Learning Administration*, *9*(4), Winter. University of West Georgia, Distance Education Center.

Hewson, M. G., Copeland, H. L., & Fishleder, A. J. (2000). What's the use of faculty development? Program evaluation using retrospective self-assessments and independent performance ratings. Proceedings from the annual meeting of the American Educational Research Association, New Orleans, April, 2000. *Teaching and Learning in Medicine*, 2001, *13*, 153–160.

Illinois Online Network (2007). *Pedagogy & learning: What makes a successful online facilitator?* Retrieved from [http://www.ion.uillinois.edu/resources/tutorials/pedagogy/instructorProfile.asp].

International Association of K–12 Online Learning (iNACOL) (2009). iNACOL national standards of quality for online courses. Retrieved from [http://www.inacol.org/research/nationalstandards/index.php].

Kearsley, G. (n.d.). Tips for training online instructors. Retrieved from [http://home.sprynet.com/~gkearsley/OItips.htm].

Keig, L., & Waggoner, M. D. (2004). Collaborative peer review: The role of faculty in improving college teaching. *ASHE-ERIC Higher Education Report*, *23-2*. Retrieved from [http://www.ntlf.com/html/lib/bib/94–2dig.htm].

Kircher, J. (2001). What are the essential characteristics of the successful online teacher and learner? Issue-oriented Dialogue White Paper, Virtual Pedagogy Conference, UW Oshkosh, July 18, 2001. Retrieved from [http://www.uwsa.edu/ttt/kircher.htm].

Levy, S. (2003). Six factors to consider when planning online distance learning programs in higher education. *Online Journal of Distance Learning Administration*, *6*(1), Spring. Retrieved from: [http://www.westga.edu/~distance/ojdla/spring61/levy61.htm].

Liao, L.-F. (2006). A flow theory perspective on learner motivation and behavior in distance education. *Distance Education*, *27*(1), 45–62.

Lorenzetti, J. P. (2009). The virtual faculty lounge: Providing online faculty development for adjunct instructors. *Best Practices for Training and Retaining Online Adjunct Faculty*, *Distance Education Report*. Retrieved from [www.FacultyFocus.com].

Lynch, R., & Dembo, M. (2004). The relationship between self-regulation and online learning in a blended learning context. *International Review of Research in Open and Distance Learning*, 5(2). Retrieved from [http://www.irrodl.org/content/v5.2/lynch-dembo.html].

Lytle, S., Lytle, V., Lenhart, K., & Skrotsky, L. (1999 Nov.-Dec.). Largescale deployment of technology-enhanced courses. *Syllabus*, pp. 57–59.

Mandernach, B. J., Donelli, E., Dailey, A., & Schulte, M. (2005). A faculty evaluation model for online instructors: Mentoring and evaluation in the online classroom. *Online Journal of Distance Education Administration*, 8(3). State University of West Georgia Distance Education Center.

Matheson, J. (2006). Strategic planning and trends in online learning. *E-articles*, August 2006. Retrieved from [http://e-articles.info/e/a/title/Strategic-Planning-and-Trends-in-Online-Education/].

Mezirow, J. (1990). *Fostering critical reflection in adulthood: A guide to transformative and emancipatory learning*. San Francisco: Jossey-Bass.

Mohono-Mahlatsi, L., & van Tonder, F. (2006). The effectiveness of mentoring in the distance teacher programme at the Lesotho college of education: Student teachers' and tutors' perceptions. *South African Journal of Education*, 26(3), 383–396.

Mooney, K. M., & Reder, M. (2008). Faculty development at small and liberal arts colleges. In D. R. Robertson & L. B. Nilson (Eds.), *To Improve the Academy: Resources for Faculty, Instructional, and Organizational Development*, 26, 158–172. San Francisco: Jossey-Bass.

Moore, A. H., Moore, J., & Fowler, S. (2009). Faculty development for the net generation. *Educause*, 6/7/09. Retrieved from [http://www.educause.edu/Resources/Educatingthe NetGeneration/FacultyDevelopmentfortheNetGen/6071].

Mullinix, B. (2008). Credibility and effectiveness in context: An exploration of the importance of faculty status for faculty developers. In D. R. Robertson & L. B. Nilson (Eds.), *To Improve the Academy: Resources for Faculty, Instructional, and Organizational Development*, 26, 173–197. San Francisco: Jossey-Bass.

National Education Association (n.d.). *Guide to teaching online courses*. Retrieved March 13, 2010 from [http://www.nea.org].

Neal, E., & Peed-Neal, I. (2009). Experiential lessons in the practice of faculty development. In L. Nilson & J. Miller (Eds.), *To Improve the Academy: Resources for Faculty, Instructional, and Organizational Development*, 27, 14–31. San Francisco: Jossey-Bass.

North American Council for Online Learning. (2009). *National standards for quality online teaching*. Retrieved from [http://www.nacol.org].

Nugent, Reardon, Smith, Rhodes, Zander, & Carter (2008). Online Learning.net, *Is online teaching for me?*, Retrieved from [http://www.onlinelearning.net/Instructor Community/selfevaluation.html].

Oomen-Early, J., & Murphy, L. (2008). Overcoming obstacles to faculty participation in distance education. *Distance Education Report*, 12(5), 4–5.

Palloff, R., & Pratt, K. (1999). *Building learning communities in cyberspace: Effective strategies for the online classroom.* San Francisco: Jossey-Bass.

Palloff, R. M., & Pratt, K. (2001). *Lessons from the cyberspace classroom: The realities of online teaching.* San Francisco: Jossey-Bass.

Palloff, R. M., & Pratt, K. (2003). *The virtual student: A profile and guide to working with online learners.* San Francisco: Jossey-Bass.

Palloff, R. M., & Pratt, K. (2005). *Collaborating online: Learning together in community.* San Francisco: Jossey-Bass.

Palloff, R. M., & Pratt, K. (2007). *Building online learning: Effective strategies for the online classroom.* San Francisco: Jossey-Bass.

Palloff, R. M., & Pratt, K. (2009). *Assessing the online learner: Resources and strategies for faculty.* San Francisco: Jossey-Bass.

Pankowski, P. (2004). Faculty training for online teaching. *T.H.E. Journal,* September 2004, Retrieved from [http://thejournal.com/articles/16956].

Pennsylvania State University & Central Florida University (2008). *Faculty self-assessment: Preparing for online teaching.* Retrieved from [http://weblearning.psu.edu/news/faculty-self-assessment].

Picciano, A. (2002). Beyond student perceptions: Issues of interaction, presence, and performance in an online course. *Journal of Asynchronous Learning Networks,* 6(1), July 2002, 21–40.

POD Network (2007). Faculty development definitions, POD Network. Retrieved from [http://www.podnetwork.org/faculty_development].

POD Network (n.d.). Ethical guidelines for faculty developers, POD Network. Retrieved from [http://podnetwork.org/faculty_development/ethicalguidelines.htm]

Preparing tomorrow's teachers to use technology (2002). Faculty development. Retrieved from [http://www.pt3.org/stories/faculty.html].

Richardson, J. C., & Swan, K. (2003). Examining social presence in online courses in relation to students' perceived learning and satisfaction. *Journal of Asynchronous Learning Networks,* 7(1), February 2003, 68–88.

Roberts, T. G., Irani, T. A., Teleg, R. W., & Lundy, L. K. (2005). The development of an instrument to evaluate distance education courses using student attitudes. *The American Journal of Distance Education,* 17(2), 77–98.

Robinson, M. A. (2003). Issues and strategies for faculty development in technology and biomedical informatics. *Advances in Dental Research* 17(34). Retrieved from [http://adr.sagepub.com/cgi/content/abstract/17/1/34].

Rovai, A. P., & Barnum, K. T. (2003). On-Line course effectiveness: An analysis of student interactions and perceptions of learning. *Journal of Distance Learning,* 18(1), 57–73.

Savery, J. (2005). Be vocal: Characteristics of successful online instructors. *Journal of Interactive Online Learning,* 4(2), 141–152. Retrieved from [http://ncolr.org/jiol].

Sherry, L., Billig, S. H., Tavalin, F., & Gibson, D. (2000). New insights on technology adoption in schools. *T.H.E. Journal,* 2/01/00. Retrieved from [http://thejournal.com/articles/2000/02/01/new-insights-on-technology-adoption-in-schools.aspx].

Stein, D., & Wanstreet, C. E. (2003). Role of social presence, choice of online or face-to-face group format, and satisfaction with perceived knowledge gained in a distance learning environment. *Midwest Research to Practice Conference in Adult, Continuing, and Community Education.* Retrieved from [http://www.alumni-osu.org/Midwest%20papers/Stein%20&%20Wanstreet—Done.pdf].

Stern, S. (2003). Professional development: Leading organizational change in community colleges. *ERIC Digests,* ERIC Clearinghouse for Community Colleges: Los Angeles. Retrieved from [http://www.eric.edu.gov].

Sweet, M., Roberts, R., Walker, J., Walls, S., Kucsera, J., Shaw, S., Riekenberg, J., & Svinicki, M. (2008). Grounded theory research in faculty development: The basis, a live example, and practical tips for faculty developers. In D. R. Robertson & L. B. Nilson (Eds.), *To Improve the Academy: Resources for Faculty, Instructional, and Organizational Development, 26,* 89–105. San Francisco: Jossey-Bass.

Taylor, A., & McQuiggan, C. (2008). Faculty development programming: If we build it, will they come? *EduCause Quarterly,* No. 3. Retrieved from [http://www.educause.edu/EDUCAUSE+Quarterly/EQVolume312008/EDUCAUSEQuarterlyMagazineVolum/163109].

Teclehaimanot, B., & Lamb, A. (2005). Technology-rich faculty development for teacher educators: The evolution of a program. *Contemporary Issues in Technology and Teacher Education, 5*(3/4), 330–344.

Tobin, T. (2004). Best practices for administrative evaluation of online faculty. *Online Journal of Distance Learning Administration, 7*(2). State University of West Georgia Distance Education Center. Retrieved from: [http://www.westga.edu/~distance/ojdla/summer72/tobin72.html].

Travis, J. E. (1995–96). Models for improving college teaching: A faculty resource. *National Teaching and Learning Forum.* Retrieved from [http://www.ntlf.com/html/lib/bib/95–6dig.htm].

Twale, D. J., & De Luca, B. M. (2008). *Faculty incivility: The rise of the academic bully culture and what to do about it.* San Francisco: Jossey-Bass.

Twigg, C. (2003). Improving learning and reducing cost: New models for online learning. *Educause Review,* September/October 2003. Retrieved from [net.educause.edu/ir/library/pdf/erm0352.pdf].

Van Dusen, C. (2009). Beyond virtual schools. *eSchool News,* Special Report, November/December 2009. Retrieved from [eSNNoveDec09SpRptBeyondVirtualSchools.pdf].

Vaughan, N. (2004). Technology in support of faculty learning communities. In M. D. Cox & L. Richlan (Eds.), *Building Faculty Learning Communities: New Directions for Teaching and Learning,* No. 97, 101–109. San Francisco: Jossey-Bass.

Velez, A. M. (2009). The ties that bind: How faculty learning communities connect online adjuncts to their virtual institutions. *Online Journal of Distance Learning Administration, 11*(2), Summer. Retrieved from [http://www.westga.edu/~distance/ojdla/summer122/velez122.html].

Vignare, K. (2009). What to expect from a virtual university. *New Directions for Higher Education*, No. 146, 97–105. San Francisco: Jossey-Bass.

Watson, J. F., & Kalmon, S. (2006). *Keeping pace with K–12 online learning: A review of state level policy and practice.* Naperville, IL: North Central Regional Educational Laboratory.

Weimer, M. G. (2002). *Learner-centered teaching: Five key changes to practice.* San Francisco: Jossey-Bass.

Weimer, M. (2009). Talk about teaching that benefits beginners and those who mentor them. *Academic Leader Special Report: 12 Tips for Improving Your Faculty Development Plan.* Retrieved from [http://www.magnapubs.com/academicleader/].

Wenger, E. (1999). *Communities of practice: Learning, meaning, and identity.* Cambridge, England: Cambridge University Press.

Williams, P. E. (2003). Roles and competencies for distance education programs in higher education institutions, *The American Journal of Distance Education, 17*(1), 45–57.

Yun, J. H., & Scorcinelli, M. D. (2009). When mentoring is the medium: Lessons learned from a faculty development initiative. In L. B. Nilson & J. E. Miller (Eds.), *To Improve the Academy: Resources for Faculty, Instructional, and Organizational Development, 27,* 365–384. San Francisco: Jossey-Bass.

Zachary, L. (2000). *The mentor's guide: Facilitating effective learning relationships.* San Francisco: Jossey-Bass.

Zhu, E. (2008). Breaking down barriers to the use of technology for teaching in higher education. In D. R. Robertson & L. B. Nilson (Eds.), *To Improve the Academy: Resources for Faculty, Instructional, and Organizational Development, 26,* 305–318. San Francisco: Jossey-Bass.

INDEX

and self-assessment, 110; and tailoring training to meet faculty needs, 105; and training for instructors at all experience levels, 105–107

"Best systems" (Hagner), 37, 104–105; and best system for developing excellent online instructors, 113–115; and best system for online faculty development, 115

Billig, S. H., 48, 49

Birch, J., 29, 30, 32, 69

Black, E. W., 78

Blackboard, xi, xii, 40

Blogs, 8, 12, 109

Boice, R., 29

Boulay, R. A., 64

Braunlich, L., 4

Bright, S., 67

Brook, C., 9

Brookfield, S., 92

Brown, A. H., 100, 101, 104, 109, 112

Byung-Ro, L., 5

C

Caffarella, R., 36, 39

California State University, Chico (CSU-Chico), 5; Rubric for Online Instruction, 5, 148

Carabajal, K., 11

Careerist faculty, 38

Carr-Chellman, A., 6

Carter, T. J., 55

Cell phones, 43, 67, 131, 135

Central Florida University, 18, 139

Certificate programs, online teaching, 60–62; resources in, 144–145; standards of, 61–62

Chamberlain, R., 9

Chaney, B. H., 11

Charalambos, V., 9

Chickering, A. W., 5

Chuang, H., 65, 66

Clay, M., 31, 32

CMS. *See* Course management system (CMS)

Collaborating Online: Learning Together in Community (Palloff and Pratt), 122, 125, 129

Collaboration, 5, 12, 26, 54, 55, 61, 67, 85, 127, 128, 155

Collura, M., 4

Commitment, 19

Communication, 19

Communication, and community building, 100–101

Community, creating, 9–10

Community, learning, 9

Community building, communication and, 100–101

Community-based approach, 54

Compassion, 19

Content category of training needs, 21, 22; for apprentice phase of development, 26; for insider phase of development, 27; for master phase of development, 28; for novice phase of development, 25; for visitor phase of development, 23

Copeland, H. L., 35

"Courageous leadership," 113

Course development: assistance with, 107–109; excellence in, 10–11

Course management system (CMS), 24, 25–26, 97, 120

Craner, J., 5

Cravener, P., 16, 17, 42, 43

Credit recovery, 80

Critical thinking, 114

Cross, K. P., 92, 128

Customization, 12

Cycles of learn, do, reflect, 39, 44

Insider phase (online faculty development), 20, 26–27; training needs for, 27

Institutional cultures, 41

Interaction, ability to promote, 12

International Association of K-12 Online Learning (iNACOL), 79

International Journal of Instructional Technology and Distance Learning, 147

International Online Conference, 145

International Review of Research in Open and Distance Learning, 147

International Society for Technology in Education (ISTE), 147

Internet search activities, 12

IPod touch, 131

Irani, T. A., 92

J

JALN. *See Journal of Asynchronous Learning Networks* (JALN)

Jamestown Community College (New York), 57

Jennings, B., 11

JOLT. *See Journal of Online Learning and Teaching* (JOLT)

Jossey-Bass Online Teaching and Learning Conference, 145

Journal of Asynchronous Learning Networks (JALN), 146

Journal of Interactive Online Learning, 147

Journal of Online Learning and Teaching (JOLT), 146

K

K–12 Teaching: becoming own faculty developer in, 86–87; and characteristics of excellent online teachers, 81–82; coping effectively with issues and challenges of, 85–86; key points in, 86;

and online teaching methods in K-12 environment, 79–81; perception gap in, 77; preparation for administration of, 84–85; preservice preparation and professional development for, 82–85; preservice teacher preparation for, 83–84; professional development for, 77–87

Kaleta, R., 11

Kalmon, S., 78

Kearsley, G., 7

Keig, L., 98, 99

Kircher, J., 6

Kling, K., 14

Kucsera, J., 35

Kursat, C., 5

L

Lamb, A., 23, 49

Lara-Alecio, R., 11

League for Innovation in the Community College, 147

Learner-focused online classroom, 92

Learners, engaging, 9–10

Learning community, 9

Learning Resources Network (LERN) Certified Online Instructor (COI) Program, 144–145

Learning Times, 143

Lecture capture software, 3, 108

Lecturing, techniques for online, 108–109

Lehman, J., 78

Lenhart, K., 108

LERN (Learning Resources Network) Certified Online Instructor (COI), 144–145

Levy, S., 53

Liao, L-F., 11

Lindemann, K., 11

Lorenzetti, J. P., 57

Lundy, L. K., 92

Online teaching: characteristics of excellent, 3–15; and engaging learners and creating community, 9–10; and excellence in course development, 10–11; and good facilitation online, 12–13; importance of establishing presence in, 7–8; and providing effective facilitation when teaching courses developed by others, 11–12

Oomen-Early, J., 101

Organization, 19

Ortegano-Layne, L., 11

P

Palloff, R. M., 5, 6, 8, 9, 11, 43, 54, 55, 109, 122, 125, 127, 129, 144, 154

Pankowski, P., xiii

"Paradoxical disjunction," 42

Park University (Missouri), 64

PBS, 87

Pedagogy: online, 82, 84; training in, theory, 57

Pedagogy category of training needs, 21; for apprentice phase of development, 26; for insider phase of development, 27; for master phase of development, 27; for novice phase of development, 25; for visitor phase of development, 23

Peed-Neal, I., 41–42

Pennsylvania State University, 18, 112, 139

Personal category of training needs, 21; for apprentice phase of development, 26; for insider phase of development, 27; for master phase of development, 27; for novice phase of development, 25; for visitor phase of development, 23

Picciano, A., 8, 9

POD (Professional and Organizational Development) Network, 17, 39, 147

Polleverywhere.com, 131, 132

PowerPoint, 3, 23, 40, 121, 130, 132; for ARS, 131

Pratt, K., 5, 6, 8, 9, 11, 43, 54, 55, 109, 122, 125–127, 144, 154

"Preparing Tomorrow's Teachers to Use Technology" (Lehman), 78

Presence: importance of establishing, 7–8; as marker of instructor excellence, 8

Preston, M., 78

Professional Certificate in Online Teaching (University of Wisconsin, Madison), 145

PT3 Program (Purdue University), 78

Purdue University, 78

Q

QOCI. *See* Quality Online Course Initiative Rubric (Illinois Online Network)

Quality Matters, 5, 61, 148; rubric, 10

Quality Online Course Initiative Rubric (Illinois Online Network), 5, 148

R

Rappaport, A., 35, 40

Reardon, R. M., 55

Reasons, S. G., 99

Reder, M., 28, 29

Reflection, 11, 50, 51, 55, 114, 127, 128, 152

"Reluctants," 38

Resources: for administrators of online programs, 149–158; faculty, 139–148; for faculty development, 119–138; in online certification programs, 144–145

Rhodes, J. A., 55

Richardson, J. C., 8

Riekenberg, J., 35

More Titles on Online Teaching & Learning From Palloff and Pratt!

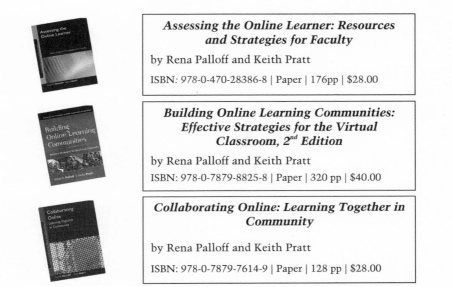

Assessing the Online Learner: Resources and Strategies for Faculty

by Rena Palloff and Keith Pratt

ISBN: 978-0-470-28386-8 | Paper | 176pp | $28.00

Building Online Learning Communities: Effective Strategies for the Virtual Classroom, 2nd Edition

by Rena Palloff and Keith Pratt

ISBN: 978-0-7879-8825-8 | Paper | 320 pp | $40.00

Collaborating Online: Learning Together in Community

by Rena Palloff and Keith Pratt

ISBN: 978-0-7879-7614-9 | Paper | 128 pp | $28.00